The

Product

of

My Selfishness

———

The Stutter and The Story

———

Matice Ahnjamine Morris

Printed in the United States of America.

ISBN-13: 978-0-692-12859-6

Matice Ahnjamine Morris
www.maticeahnjamine.com

Cover photography by Patrick Lanham
www.patricklanhamphoto.com

Cover design by Brittney Roseburrow
www.unpredictabledesigns.com

Contents

Title Page

Copyright

Dedication

Foreword

Acknowledgments

About the Author

To the woman who gave me my roots—

My momma, Denita

and

To the man who gave me my wings—

My pops, Wade Sr.

Foreword by Bonnie McKenzie M.S., CCC-SLP, BRS-FD

Speech Pathologist/Board Certified Fluency Specialist

As this book is being published, there are over 3.5 million people who stutter in the United States and about 70 million worldwide. Best research efforts point to a neurodevelopmental cause of their impediment. Stuttering is *not* due to nervousness, being tickled as a baby, overly strict parents or any of the other myths you may have heard. The multitude of misconceptions about stuttering may contribute to the stigma most people who stutter experience. Stuttering is a complex speech disorder and while it may have neurological beginnings, it is complicated and often worsened by the very reactions and stress it creates for the individual who stutters.

Stuttering can be observed by the physical manifestations of blocking, repeating and prolonging sounds. It can be accompanied by a wide variety of physical signs of struggle such as facial grimacing as the speaker attempts to push the words out. But a huge part of stuttering is experienced on the *inside*. The fear, anticipation, internal dialog and struggle that exists within the individual who stutters is not always seen by others. Imagine the tension that rises in the speech muscles as the person who stutters senses that the listener is drawing conclusions that there is "something wrong" with the speaker. Imagine the humiliation and frustration felt when the listener offers simplistic advice such as, "take your time," "slow down," or "just relax."

Research has noted that stuttering begins as a neurophysiological issue but is perpetuated and worsened by those internal reactions. As one adult client stated, "No matter how it started, I feel like, today, I stutter because I fear I will stutter." The more the child who stutters fears stuttering or tries "not to stutter," the more he or she will tend to stutter. It is often at a young age that children who stutter begin to express this fear. Three-year-olds will sometimes tell a parent, "Mommy, I can't say it." Many a seven- or eight-year-old has told me, "I was afraid I wouldn't be able to ask the teacher to go to the bathroom and ended up asking to borrow a pencil." Lots of older kids have shared that they were convinced they were the only person who stutters. Adults often say the fear of not being able to say their own name haunts them. Often a person who stutters will go to great lengths to hide their stutter. One adult client actually gave the name of his competitor's business when he was caught off guard and couldn't say his own. Avoiding speaking situations, using different words, or camouflaging the stuttering may seem on the surface to be a great solution—to the "non-stutterer." However, these "solutions" often just lead to more fear and more struggle. A common complaint of a person who stutters is "I want to be able to say what I want to say!"

Many people who stutter work with a speech pathologist. Many are active in self-help organizations such as NSA (National Stuttering Association), Friends, ISA (International Stuttering Association) and other organizations, such as Stuttering Foundation, which seek to assist people who stutter, their families, and professionals who work with those who stutter. And of course, many go it alone. Some find just the right mix to help them minimize the effects of stuttering. For some who stutter, the speech difficulty is an annoyance. For others, it affects every aspect of life and every decision they make.

In my work with people who stutter of every age, the focus is on two broad areas: the physical or mechanical aspects of speech AND reducing the underlying reactions of fear, anticipation, negative thoughts and beliefs that tend to make the problem worse.

Learning to manage the physical aspects of speech is no easy task. Over 100 muscles are involved in the initiation of speech. Coordination among exhaled breath or the outward flow of air, the vocal folds coming together across the stream of air to begin vibration (what we refer to as voicing), and the mechanics of the articulators to produce various speech sounds is necessary to create speech. This process occurs naturally for most of us, with only occasional blips. In the case of stuttering, the muscles themselves are not impaired, and sometimes (even most of the time), the speech system operates without a hitch. However, during stuttering, the vocal folds seemingly slam shut, blocking the airflow necessary to initiate vibration or voicing. Understanding speech production in order to work with the flow instead of fighting against it can be helpful. Learning to manage the speech muscles while thinking about what you're saying in "real-life" speaking situations and in the face of fear is challenging to say the least.

Most fluency experts agree that "acceptance" of stuttering and even making friends with the stutter by demystifying and desensitizing it is a critical first step for the person who stutters. Self-disclosure or becoming more open about stuttering with others can be a big part of this process. Talking about the very thing the person has attempted to hide his or her whole life usually requires a great deal of courage. Facing that fear and making friends with stuttering has led some to actually seeing stuttering as a "gift."

While there is a wealth of shared experiences, each person who stutters is unique and has his or her own story, his or her own journey with stuttering. Researchers will tell you that people who stutter are no different from people who don't stutter—except that they stutter. In my 30-plus years of specializing in the treatment of stuttering, I have met and worked with thousands of people who stutter. I would tell you that people who stutter are among the bravest, finest, and most inspirational people I've ever met. Perhaps it is this journey of dealing with a stutter that produces such talented and amazing people.

I worked with Matice for only a few sessions, but I could immediately tell that she was one of those courageous and inspirational people. I know her story will fascinate her readers!

When I do anything, it is usually with other people in mind, trying to please them in an effort to atone for any inconvenience my stuttering may cause. Even as I began contemplating this book, I fretted about what readers would think. Then I realized that in order to be completely vulnerable in my story, to really come from a place of honesty, I had to have a moment of pure selfishness. I had to think only about myself. Those times that I felt myself beginning to write to please the world, I stopped . . . to please myself. I had to write for me, as if I were the only one to ever read this book. And that is what I have done. This is the product of my selfishness!

CHAPTER ONE

Fluency: My Younger Years

I did not always stutter. I know it is impossible to remember life before a certain age, but I know I was not born with a stutter. That is probably the most intriguing thing to this day: That I did not start talking with this life-changing speech impediment. When I hear other people tell their story, they always say how they have been stuttering since they first began talking. That was not the case for me, as my involvement with speech therapy did not begin until the first grade. I went to a speech teacher because I could not pronounce my R's, or so everyone thought. The catch? I *could* pronounce my R's.

At that time, my older brother, Wade, was Captain Hero in my eyes. Anything he did, I wanted to do. If he peed standing up, I wanted to pee standing up. If it was smoldering hot in the summertime and he wanted to prance around with no shirt on, I, too, wanted to prance around with no shirt on. Much to his annoyance, I was always fast on his heels growing up, doing everything he should (as well as should not) have been doing. So, when he started going to speech therapy because he could not pronounce his R's, I figured I would join him. I made sure I could not pronounce my R's either. Unbeknownst to my parents, I started acting as though it was difficult for me to say a hard R sound. "Really" turned in to "weally," "very" turned into "vewwy," and just like that I was put into speech therapy, the same as my big brother. The stuttering did not come until later, two years to be exact.

There is not a particular time that I remember my stuttering beginning, but my father and I had conversations later in life in which he said he thought the divorce between him and my mother was when my stuttering took root.

My mom, dad, brother, and I lived in a house in Freeport, Illinois. You've probably never heard of Freeport. It's a small town in northern Illinois where everyone knows everyone—and everyone's business—and Wal-Mart is the meet-up spot. To this day I dread going to Wal-Mart in Freeport because everyone will recognize my mom and say, "Hey, Denita!" and a trip to grab toilet paper and candy turns into a community reunion. Yes, it is that small of a town!

Despite Freeport being a small town, while living there during my youngest years, I had no complaints. My mom was a school teacher. She had an affinity for kids. As I write this, she is one school year away from retiring. She had Wade when she was 23 and me two years later, at 25. I remember when the three of us used to take evening walks around the neighborhood, something you cannot get her to do now because exercise is just . . . too much. My dad was a public defender, and when he was not dealing with accused criminals, he would teach Wade and me how to ride bikes in the parking lot of our complex. Another activity I remember was how Wade and I would rally the neighborhood kids and play in the yard where there was this ancient tree with long, low branches that formed a tent-like secret-hiding place where we would go to "make believe." In other words, a typical childhood.

It became atypical in 1994 when one day my brother and I halted our playing upstairs and we decided to come halfway down the steps and peek around the wall to see into the living room. Momma was standing there with her back to the stairs; she was facing two cops who were also there in the living room. My father was going from the basement to his car with all his belongings, crossing through the living room each time as he was grabbing everything. I did not quite understand what was going on, as I was only five at the time. But I do remember crying because even in the innocence of childhood, you know when something is wrong, even if why it is wrong is still a mystery.

My brother and I knew not to make a sound, but I am sure everyone saw our beady eyes peeking around the stairwell. When the cops and my dad left, I remember Momma sitting at the bottom of the steps. I went down and laid my head in her lap and asked with tears in my eyes, "When is Daddy coming back?" While he had not left my life, he had left our home. Life as a two-biological-parent household as I knew it was over.

It was not until recently (in 2016) that I realized this scene from my childhood has shaped many decisions in my relationships, whether they be with female friends or with dating a man. I had always been comfortable and easy letting female friends go because I had my mom there for me at the bottom of the stairs. And I always held on to men because I did not want the situation with my dad's moving out to happen in my dating life with a guy walking out on me. It was these defining moments, including the subsequent divorce of my parents, that my father came to believe marked the commencement of my stuttering. Children deal with traumatic events in unique ways. Having my parents' divorce when I was young, coupled with a pre-disposition in my bloodline via my maternal grandmother's cousin and my father, both of whom stuttered, my dad's belief may not have been too far off.

The three years after my parents' split were a blur, though both were present in my brother's and my life. Although my father moved to Aurora, the Chicago suburb about 100 miles away from Freeport, with his girlfriend turned wife, Julie, Wade and I would always visit. My mom's boyfriend turned husband, Wendell, moved into the house in Freeport.

In 1997, Wendell, by now my stepfather, accepted a pastoral position in St. Louis. Thus, this position would require a move. We packed up everything in Illinois and made the five-hour trek to Missouri, a move that would years later reveal that people do not always present their true identities.

CHAPTER TWO

First Stutter

I do not remember the first time I stuttered, but I remember the first time I knew my stuttering was a problem. It was in the fourth grade at Rose Acres Elementary School, in Mrs. Rice's class, and I was called upon to read aloud. I suppose somewhere within my psyche, I knew I already had a speech issue (but the thought had not really taken root) because in that moment I remember trying to look away so she would not see me. Kind of like how my dog, King, looks away when he knows he should not be in the kitchen watching me eat. He figures that if he looks away and cannot see me, then surely, I cannot see him. That is how I figured it would work with Mrs. Rice. My thinking seemed logical to me at the time as a fourth grader. Certainly, I would get a pass! So much for the pass and for such tomfoolery. Of course, she saw me, and she called on me. The rest is yet another blur. All I remember after that was getting out maybe a few words before the whole class broke out in gut-busting laughter. Literally, from that moment till my freshman year in college, I made sure I never had to speak in front of a large group or read aloud again.

In dealing with the early stages of my stuttering (and truthfully, even as the years progressed), my parents had polar opposite approaches. My mom's approach was the nurturing, protective, "you are not going to mess with my baby" approach. It probably had something to do with her being an elementary school teacher and her kinship with children. Her approach was softer compared to my dad's. She would speak up for me and answer questions for me when I got a hard block, or could not get the word out. We got so in tune over the years that all I would have to do was make the slightest motion and she would know to answer for me. The fact that she always knew what I was trying to say when it was her turn to speak up for me was (and is) testament to how in sync we became over the years with my stutter.

When I turned 18, that synchronization was never truer than when my church, Washington Tabernacle Missionary Baptist Church, awarded me a scholarship based on grades, community involvement, and overall character. It was the Nance Scholarship, established by members of our church. On the Sunday the scholarship recipients were announced, the host of the scholarship committee stood at a microphone and stated that each recipient would have to announce where they went to high school and where they would be attending college. No sooner were these words spoken than I had a panic attack. This was not a trivial, oh-my-goodness moment. This was a full-fledged freak-out, an "I have just received a guilty verdict and am about to go to the gas chamber" death sentence. I guess a little "gas chamber" got inside of me in that instant because I went from passing gas, to my hands and face sweating, to my eyes burning with tears, to uncontrollable shakes that could not be stopped—even with the assistance of the Almighty.

Without hesitation, my mom took one look at me and said, "I will go up and say it for you." She gave me my roots. I once read that one parent usually gives their child roots and one parent gives their child wings. That tender, loving care that came from my mom's wanting to nurture and protect me from any hurt that could come from others due to my stuttering, was her giving me my roots. I compare it to nurturing a plant's roots for it to blossom into a beautiful lily.

If I am going to tell this story truthfully, I am going to tell the entire truth—my truth with total transparency. Even to this day, in my late 20s, I still have my mom call to make my doctor and hair appointments. If I need to phone a call center, I write down all the information I think she will need. We sit there together on speakerphone, her speaking for me and me being a pest trying to tell her what to say. Could I make these calls myself? Yes. Have I made these calls myself? Yes. But the stress of these phone calls makes my stuttering worse. When you have been hung up on or had people think the reception is bad because your speech is so spotty, it becomes a "by any means necessary" situation.

The first time I was ever hung up on was during a call to a store to determine their hours of operation while hanging at my dad's office for "Take Your Daughter to Work Day". He was a lawyer, and I looked forward to skipping school every year to spend this time with him. This leads me to the topic of his response to my stuttering. His approach to my stuttering was hard knocks, which made sense as he defended criminals on a daily basis. He was also a military vet with years of service reminding him of such verities as the power of mind over matter. If I needed to make a call, I knew better than to ask him. I cannot remember a single occasion where he ever made a phone call on my behalf, unless it was something serious where, as a child, I could not call myself. If I was trying to get a word out, he would coax me to relax, but he would never bail me out by saying what he knew was next. I may not have seen the whole staircase of how my stuttering would turn out and how it would affect people, but my dad allowed me to take the next step (or word, in this instance) on my own to figure out the effects of my stuttering for myself. He nurtured my growth through my freedom to stutter, instead of bailing me out during a block. Similar to taking a leap of faith, he gave me my wings.

While I lived in St. Louis with my mom and stepdad during second through the fifth grade, my stuttering got progressively worse. I was still a child, and it is understood that children have a sense of urgency in everything they do. If they need to get somewhere, they run to their destination. Parents are always telling their children to slow down. That was the case with my stuttering. Instead of running with my legs, I was running with my words. I was in so much of a rush that I could only get out one or two words at a time. This was the period in my life when my stuttering was at its worst. It was around this time that my mom took me to see some doctors to have my speech evaluated. One doctor in particular thought I had Tourette syndrome (TS).

Tourette syndrome is a type of neurological disorder characterized by repetitive, involuntary movements and vocalizations called tics, according to the National Institute of Health.

During this discovery period, talk-shows like "Maury" and "Jerry Springer" were popular. It just so happened that an episode aired on one of the shows featuring people who had TS. One boy was cussing out his mom and the mom, at times, was laughing at his outbursts. At that time (I was around 8 or 9) I did not really understand what I was watching; I just knew that if I said the things to my momma that that boy was saying to his, I would be in a heap of trouble, and stuttering would be the least of my worries.

That was my introduction to Tourette's, via a television show, where everything is exaggerated for maximum dramatic effect. That very exaggeration was what my father displayed when he heard that I had been diagnosed with TS. He had zero tolerance for the diagnosis. I think it was more of his not wanting to make this stuttering situation more than what it already was. As a man, his natural response to a problem was to fix it, but this was not something he could fix. My speech impediment was out of his control. Sometimes it seemed to even make him uncomfortable. Beyond it being something he could not fix, he blamed himself for the cause of the issue, namely, the divorce.

I have countless memories of being in public and hearing him over my shoulder in a hushed voice saying, "Relaaaaaaaax" or "Breeeeeeathe." On occasion, if I was taking entirely too long, he would tell me to stop. He would inhale, as an example for me to follow suit. Then, he would tell me to try getting my words out again. I would somehow always manage to succeed following his assistance, to which he would reply with a self-satisfied grin, "See what happens when you use your techniques?"

To my father, I may have had some quirks, but he never thought of them as tics. I do not know if I ever called them tics, either, but I do recall many rapid movements as a child and even into my adult years. The time when I had the most-recognizable tics was when my mom, my stepfather, and I all went to Oklahoma for a few days to visit his side of the family.

I remember blinking non-stop during the entire trip, clearing my throat and sniffling as though I had the flu. All of these actions occurred when I was not speaking. Whenever I tried to talk, I would tap on my knee in an effort to get the words out. The blinking and tapping were not all involuntary because I could have stopped them if I wanted to. The tapping was more an unconscious effort on my part to help tease words out. I will never forget sitting in the living room and my mom explaining to members of my step-dad's family that I had tics.

To this day, I have some tendencies that could be mistaken as tics. However, the one factor differentiating my speech antics is that tics are not controllable. My tics were controllable. Still, there are times when I put great effort into holding my foot or hand still to fight the urge to tap.

I get so tense from restraining myself sometimes, that I am exhausted by the time the strain of the speaking situation is over. Though I still find myself blinking a lot, even if I am not trying to speak, I can control it. To a non-stutterer (reading this) it may seem strange. Curiosity may even cause you to wonder: If it can be controlled, then why do you blink so much? The answer is this: It is complicated. I can only explain the blinking as an urge. I get the *urge* to blink non-stop. The same goes for when I speak: I get the urge to tap. If my hands are visible, I try to control the tap, but then it gets harder to get my words out. In this instance, I will tap, sometimes even jerk, my foot on the ground to get the words out. If I place my hands below a table or out of the listener's line of vision, I resume my tapping to get the words out. Sometimes I tap into thin air, sometimes I tap my knees. The block I feel between my lips or in the back of my throat when I stutter causes me to want to keep momentum going elsewhere in my body in order to resume speaking. Sometimes it works, other times it does not.

Using the phone, especially when I am not familiar or comfortable with the person at the other end, is one of my top-three worst stuttering scenarios. The other person cannot see my movements and facial expressions; thus, they cannot get distracted. In order to continue a conversation, they have to be listening to my voice alone. That fact is *always* on my mind. Since I stutter so badly on the phone, I try to use techniques that could be considered tics most of the time. This is why I do not like answering the phone around people. If you could see me on the phone in those moments, you would wonder if I had a condition far beyond "just" a stutter. I tend to jump up and down in order to get a word out. I bounce around and lunge, slap my stomach and tap my head. There have been times when I have even lost my breath because I am not breathing while trying to get the word out but am still doing all these physical movements, which eventually exhausts me. I have broken out in a sweat—sounding as if I just finished a marathon because I could not breathe.

With the high anxiety of phone calls, in the event I have to make a call myself, I try to anticipate every part of the conversation before it occurs. Mentally, I create a script. For words that I know will cause me to block, I substitute other words. Blocking words are most often words that begin with a letter that is pronounced with an initially closed mouth, such as "m" and "b," e.g., money and bird. Even saying my name, Matice, is difficult, so introductions to people tend to have them ask, "You don't remember your name" due to my long pause. Typically, I reply and let them know I stutter, but one day I am going to jokingly maintain a straight face, say, "Actually, no, I don't remember," and just walk away. I practice on my name and other hard words and try to hum to relax my vocal chords. I give myself a sort of pep talk and reassure myself that whoever is on the other end, they will just have to be patient. If I have never met the person, I remind myself that I never have to see them again. The annoying encouragement that strangers often give me, I say to myself: "It is OK." Because it is. All this mental exertion for a routine task that is second nature to a fluent speaker is a source of great stress to a stutterer. Stress only amplifies the stutter in the proverbial vicious circle.

My dad saw rather early that my speech impediment was going to be a problem for me. When my mom and step-father moved to St. Louis, we stayed in a parsonage in Normandy, a St. Louis suburb. Wade and I always went to visit my dad for the summer or on any long break we had. Eventually, I was the only one making the trip because Wade later went to live with him—a decision that made sense because my brother and stepfather were not friendly by any stretch of the imagination.

I remember sitting in my pop's kitchen during one of my visits and his telling me if I lived with him I would be in speech therapy. At the time—I was about 9 or 10—I could barely put two words together without stuttering. By now, my disfluency was at its worst. In late elementary and throughout middle school, my stutter was more pronounced and extremely difficult. I suspect that was because I had internalized my dad's desire to "fix" my speech, and his pending proposal to enroll me in speech therapy had made me not only more aware of my stutter, but very self-conscious it, too. I would try so intently not to stutter around him that I would stutter more. The pressure he put on me from an early age about my stuttering let me know he was always focusing on my stuttering whenever I talked. So, of course, I was always focused on my stuttering whenever I talked around him. At the same time, it made me proud when he would acknowledge that I was improving, and I would try so hard to keep that momentum going. However, I soon came to realize that patience was not his strong suit. He would get frustrated if I did not use my techniques, leaving me feeling the sting of failure when he would not recognize my improvement.

With stuttering, there are days my lack of fluency is so frustrating that it feels as if I am in a trench, deep as the Earth's core. Then there are those days I am so fluent that I am as high as a mountain reaching to the moon. Sometimes I have days when I cannot say much of anything without a stutter. Other days, the words flow so easily that people would never think I have a speech impediment.

CHAPTER THREE

G-G-Growing Up

When my dad and Julie were having their first child, I decided I wanted to go live with them. They had moved to Rockford, a city about 45 minutes from Freeport and about an hour and a half from Aurora. After they moved to Rockford, Celene was born, in January 2000. My little brother Tyson was born a couple of years later, the day after I turned 13, in February 2002. Now my dad had all four of his children under the same roof. Sure enough, as soon as I was under said roof, my pops held true to his word and I started speech therapy.

I hated it! But he was adamant about it, and he was spending his money for it, so I went. One thing about my dad was he did not like to waste money. He called it being economically wise; I called it being cheap. Actually, cheap is being generous. That aside, he expected to see a noticeable improvement in my speech. Considering the fact that I stutter to this day, I wonder if he thinks he wasted his money. I am sure he saw it as an investment in my future, but I cannot help but compare him to Chris's dad in the television sitcom, "Everybody Hates Chris." Both are tall, dark skinned and bald headed. Neither of them likes to spend money. Chris's dad counted down to the penny when a light was left on and no one was in the room: "That's $2.67 worth of electricity!" The same went for my dad. Each block of a word was worth a nickel toward the cost of a therapy session. Jokingly, of course.

Every technique I have learned came from my speech pathologist at Rockford Memorial Hospital, Mrs. Oliveri. I went to see her twice a week in the mornings, for about an hour each time, before school started for the day. She taught me that if I began making an H sound before I said what I needed to say, it would help ease out words. "H" opens the throat, which is vital to a stutterer. She also taught me to "sing" my words. My mom has always suggested this as well. To a middle-school-aged child, dealing with other middle-school-aged children who were not familiar with stuttering but who were quite familiar with cracking jokes, how comfortable would it have been to turn my life into a constant musical? Not very. But the interesting thing is I never stutter when I sing. That is common in a lot of, if not all, stutterers. The constant flow of air that is required when singing makes it that much easier to be fluent and maintain that fluency. Mrs. Oliveri also taught me to breathe. As ingrained as you would think this is, I constantly have to tell myself to let go of a word I am trying to force out and start again. When I am trying to force a word out, I am not breathing, so there is zero air flow in my nose or mouth. In my younger years and even now, a lot of my conversations end with my being out of breath if I am excited or in a hurry. Breathing was the one technique that my dad constantly impressed upon me.

I remember one incident in particular where my pops took it upon himself to remind me to breathe at a very awkward moment. In the summer of 2015 (I was 26 at the time), my dad, Julie, Celene, Tyson and I went to a family reunion in Atlanta. (Wade had long been in the Air Force and married with two kids, so he was not able to make it this particular year.) After the reunion ended, it was time to check out of the hotel. My dad checked out of his room first, then I stepped up to the counter—and BLOCK! I could not get a single word out. The woman at the front desk was looking back and forth at my father and me like, "Is she going to talk?" Then she realized I was stuttering because I was getting noises out, just not words. My face was also contorting as it normally does when I am trying to force a word out. My dad took it upon himself to say out loud, in front of her, "Breeeeeathe," in an unnecessarily elongated breath. Captain Copycat, aka the front-desk attendant, joined in with him and let out her own breath, saying, "It's OK." I stopped even trying to talk until she decided to stop being as dramatic as my dad. The look on my face must have been one of "I am smiling, but you are irritating my entire soul" because my dad let out a chuckle and was telling Captain

Copycat he knew how annoyed I could get. Given all my years of experience with him at this point in my life, I was used to his shenanigans. That was the last time he ever expressed his desire for me to stop stuttering.

In speech therapy, Mrs. Oliveri would have me make phone calls to stores, and that was probably the most stressful part of my time with her. The simple calls she would have me make, such as calling stores and asking their hours, or calling to see if they had a certain product, were extremely challenging. When I was not in therapy and had to make calls for myself, I remember one time asking my dad to make a call for me and he refused. I knew from that point on never to ask him to make a call. He was not going to enable the very thing he so desperately wanted me to get rid of. My mom, though, made, and still makes, some of my calls when it has to do with business and it is important to me for people on the other end of the line to know that my stuttering does not affect my mental capabilities. It is embarrassing, but it is real. She helps me out, for example, when I have to dispute a bill or something of that nature. Some people equate stuttering with a mental disability and would try to get one over; I am well aware of that. Mom is there to make sure that does not happen.

Years later, on Valentine's Day in 2014, I went to visit a friend in New York. He asked me to make a phone call to a Chinese restaurant to see if they delivered on a Sunday. He did not know that I had not made a blind call like that in years. I did not want to tell him that I, at 25 years of age, could not make a phone call, but I also did not want to stress myself out making the call. After some minutes, I walked out of the living room and into his room where I would be alone. I made the call. I did it. I walked back out and told him the truth about my calling phobia. The pride I felt in making the call far outweighed the embarrassment I felt in admitting I had been scared to do it. Even so, it would be years before I fully conquered my fear of using the phone.

Speech therapy in middle school was probably more of a struggle for the counselor than it was for me. I did it to appease my dad, of course, and I only put minimal effort into it. At that age, I wanted to fit in, not stick out. I would sneak into the therapist's office when it was time for my session and sneak out at the end so no one saw me coming or going. I fancied myself the Stealthy Stutterer. At this time, I was also going to speech therapy at the doctor's office, kind of like two-a-day except it was two-a-week. I am sure my dad was in heaven.

Speech therapy in middle school was a repeat of the techniques I learned from Mrs. Oliveri at the hospital. The only difference was school opened up the world of speeches and public speaking. I once heard that people's biggest fear is not death or snakes or anything of that nature. Their biggest fear is public speaking. People would rather be bitten by a poisonous snake and die than speak in front of a large group. That says a lot. Our fears, the things that keep us up at night, are mental, pure and simple, not actual threats to our physical well-being.

This stuttering of mine is always more pronounced around people, in front of groups, and in unknown situations. It has led me to confront the possibility that my stuttering is the result of my perceptions and nothing more. If I change the way I think about my stuttering, if I change my thoughts and get rid of my fears, can I get rid of my stuttering?

The speeches I had to give in middle school were always modified for me. Instead of standing in front of the whole class, I was allowed to pick three or four students to go to my speech therapy class, and I would give the speech in front of them. I always chose close friends. Even around people I was comfortable with, I stuttered when all eyes were on me.

All through middle school, I worked adamantly on improving my stutter. I would have speech therapy at home through my dad's frustrating yet repeated reminders. He would have me read aloud for 30 minutes. I would go to the hospital for speech therapy and afterward have therapy again at school. Then, in seventh grade, everything changed. On Sept. 11, 2001, the Twin Towers were hit. I remember being in my dad's car that morning on the way to school because I had just completed therapy at the hospital. On the way, we listened to the radio. I really had no idea what was going on, as, being only 12, I was not quite processing the significance of how the events of the day had unfolded. It was not until I got to band class that I began to really understand what was going on.

We did not play our instruments that day. Mr. Collins, my teacher, had a TV on a cart and it was pulled out from the wall. The news was on. While we were watching, he was explaining how terrorists had hit the Twin Towers with two planes. He went on to explain that a war was possible and even highly likely, and that the army would be deployed overseas to go fight. I knew my dad was in the army. I knew he went away one weekend a month, and I knew, or thought I knew, there was a possibility that he would have to go fight. I remember sitting in the brown metal chair in class and crying. I envisioned him getting shot, and I thought of the possibility of his death. By the time class was over and I was on to my next class, I was calmer but still nervous and anxious that he would have to go to war.

Soon enough, my fears were confirmed and my dad was deployed to the Middle East. He was there for a total of eighteen months. During this time, I lived with my stepmom, who had her hands full with Tyson (who was still a baby), Celene (a toddler), and Wade and me (two teenagers who were full of mischief and attitude). In my younger years, my attitude was terrible. That was to be expected between a stepdaughter and a stepmom, I guess, especially at thirteen years old.

I finished middle school and was spending the summer in St. Louis with my mom. While there, I made up my mind that I was going to stay in St. Louis for good and start high school there. I remember specifically one day I was in the library because my mom was adamant about our educating ourselves over the summer. We got to watch about an hour of TV a day, and the rest of the time we had to read, play outside, or occupy our minds ourselves without the aid (or distraction, my mother would say) of a television. So, visits to the library were as second nature as breathing. I was using a computer one day and my dad called my mom's cell phone. I got on the phone and was talking to my dad, who by this time knew I wanted to stay in St. Louis and live with my mom. He said, "I have some good news that could persuade you to move back to Rockford. If I tell you, will you come back?" I said, "No", but he told me anyway: his deployment was over, and he would be coming back to the States.

That phone call was indicative of my personality and the struggle that always ensued with my father and me in dealing with my stuttering. Even though I was young, I was very headstrong. I knew what I wanted, even at a young age, and I was not going to be easily swayed. Our interactions with my stuttering were similar. He wanted me to not stutter and he would try to pressure me with my techniques and slowing down, breathing and relaxing. I, on the other hand, was dead set on doing things my way, which, essentially, meant learning from my mistakes. We were both stubborn to the core. But the decision had been made, and I started high school in St. Louis.

Since Mom was a teacher, I went to school in the district where she worked, even though it was not the district in which I lived. I got an individualized education program, or IEP, for short. The school's counselor/speech therapist assessed my impediment and together with Mom and me, she figured out a way to incorporate speech therapy into my schedule.

During my freshman year, I went to speech therapy faithfully. We decided that prior to the first day of class, the counselor would let all of my teachers know that I stuttered. The biggest fear I always had on the first day of class was introductions. I remember my first class was health with Mrs. McGhee. Of course, we had to introduce ourselves. Because I had an IEP, I would always try to talk to the teacher before class began. I would rush to class to talk to them before most of the class came in the room. That would ensure some privacy. Sometimes I had to talk to the teacher in hushed tones a minute or two after class was supposed to begin with the other students sitting there wondering why I was holding everything up. That probably was not their actual thought, but that was my thought since I was so self-conscious.

I would always tell the teacher I stuttered and ask if they were going to have us introduce ourselves. If they said yes, I would say I was not comfortable with that. Some teachers would introduce me themselves when the time came for me to speak; others would direct the next student to talk instead and skip me, while kids sat there wondering why I was not talking. While these approaches "solved" the problem to some extent, they left me feeling uncomfortable.

I remember very specifically my first day of high school when it came to lunch time. Half of the day was over and that meant I only had a few more classes to go before the awkward introductions to my teachers and classmates would be over. But lunch brought a struggle all its own. Since moving back to St. Louis, I really did not remember too many people. The few I did remember, I was not best friends with to say the least. My school had three lunches and, naturally, I was on the lunch where I did not recognize anyone from my elementary years. So, I went through the line and got my lunch, trying to concoct a plan of what to do. I wanted to sit with people so I would not be alone, but I was too scared to walk up to a group of complete strangers and ask if

I could sit with them. They would try to get to know me, and I would not be able to hide my stuttering with all attention on me. Nor, in the alternative, did I want to sit at an empty table and look "uncool." After weighing my options, for the first week of high school, I ate lunch in the bathroom right outside the lunchroom. Looking back, that was probably the most unsanitary choice (and no, I would never do that now), but in high school, fear reigns over common sense. By the second week, I decided I would branch out. I figured I could not spend every single lunch of the entire school year in the bathroom. Come that next Monday, I saw another black girl sitting alone at a table. Perfect. I always did better one on one than in group situations, anyway.

When people are alone, like that girl in the lunchroom sitting at the table, they are less likely to feed off the energy of someone else and less likely to make someone—me with my stutter—feel embarrassed. My thought processes and experiences from the time I was young were that people are more compassionate and less prone to tease when they are alone and faced with an unusual and awkward situation than in groups, so I used that to my advantage.

I do not remember the name of that girl, I do not have my yearbook, and I do not care to use Facebook to creep and figure out her name. Though we sat together my freshman year the whole first semester, we never really became friends and barely talked other than sharing basic, short information such as our names and classes. On days she was not at the table, I went back to the bathroom, because since no one else ever sat at our table, I would be alone if I sat there.

Eventually, I mustered up enough courage to sit alone. I was tired of hiding out in the bathroom.

The first time I sat at the table alone, I held in tears. I felt lonely, but I stayed. By the second semester, I had made two friends, Patience and Brittani. Luckily, we all had the same lunch. After that first semester of freshman year, I never ate in the bathroom again. Through my friendships with Patience and Brittani, I made other friends, and I also became acquainted with more people from my classes. Just putting myself out there was all it took. If I had never had the courage to sit alone at the table or the courage to walk up and ask the people in my classes if I could eat with them, I would also have been alone that second semester.

By sophomore year, I was more confident in my friendships and myself. I made less time to go to speech therapy though I still went in the beginning because I was not confident enough to introduce myself while stuttering. I knew people knew about my stuttering, but I also knew the maturity level of high-schoolers. At the end of the day, I was not going to be laughed at by an entire class as though I were in the in the fourth grade all over again. Kids grow up, yes, but they are not grown enough in high school, so I remained on high alert.

My junior year I stopped going to my speech therapist completely. By my senior year, I did not even think to go. My senior year was when I had speech class and the student teacher stuttered. I had never considered any type of job where I would have to stand in front of people to speak, except when I worked at McDonalds for about two months during my sophomore year and never went back because the guy flipping burgers stressed me out. Even then, I only had to talk to whoever was in front of me placing their order, and only reply with their total and a thank you. It was pretty straightforward compared to having to teach a class.

      I would sacrifice my left baby toe rather than teach a bunch of high-schoolers with my obvious stutter that effectively introduced me before I even spoke (only because I could not get my first words out sometimes). But here he was (I cannot remember his name), teaching oral communications to a bunch of high-schoolers. I thought it was really cool. The class got used to him, so his stutter did not become an issue. However, my stutter did. This was a class for giving speeches, and I freaked out. So, as in middle school when I gave my speeches to a small group in my speech therapy class, I gave my speeches to the student teacher. I thought that would calm my nerves, having a fellow stutterer be the audience, but it did not. My fear was there regardless. Again, I wondered if I stuttered because of the impediment or because of the anxiety. The mind is far stronger than we realize. My expectation of stuttering and the potential negative reaction from others—then and now—may be what is still keeping me stuttering, more than the actual condition itself.

CHAPTER FOUR

Stutter Bae: Dating With a Stutter

A guy I dated accompanied me to church one Sunday and, unbeknownst to me, was listening intently as I read aloud a Bible passage in unison with the congregation. As we left church, he said, "You do not stutter when you read aloud." I corrected him, saying, "I do not stutter when I speak in unison with other people." He told me that my stuttering was not normal. But what is normal? In life and in our interactions with people, normal is relative and subjective. And "normal" is definitely defined by our own standards when it comes to dating.

I cannot really say dating started for me in high school because even though I liked guys back then, they did not reciprocate that same interest. I was awkward with the whole stutter situation that presented itself in my speech. That made me shy. Super shy. I was also taller than most of the boys my age. It had been that way since middle school, and though I was used to it, that did not mean I liked it. When sophomore year of high school rolled around I realized the boys were starting to get taller, and the upperclassmen were already taller. A whole new world was opened up for me.

Two of my friends outside of school, Niecy and Michella, were the first friends I made when I moved back to St. Louis. They knew how important it was for me to have a tall guy. Whenever we all hung out with guys, they knew to ask for a tall friend to come along because a shorty was not an option. I was always advanced in my dating as far as my standards and what I expected. I wanted to feel protected by a man. If I were taller than he, I would feel I had to protect him, as a sort of mother figure. That is not attractive, so I never gave shorter guys the time of day. Numerous guys have tried, and some have even asked why this is so. Back in my early 20s, Patience and I, along with some other friends, went out to a club. We were dancing and having a good time when a short guy came up and tried his luck. I tried to pass on him so as not to hurt his feelings, but he persisted, asking me why I was not interested. Being the type of person who was blunt, did not lie, and had not yet learned the art of diplomacy, I said, "It is because you are short." How quick I was to judge this man for something out of his control, yet I did not want anyone to judge me for my stuttering, which I also could not control at times, even when using my techniques. Nevertheless, out of all that, I have not changed: I still will not date a short man.

I liked a few guys throughout my high school years. Because of my stuttering, there were many moments of awkward silence. I liked this one guy named JJ. My crush on him began when I went to visit my mom in St. Louis, and before I moved back. He was one of the young people at my mom's church, where she was the Youth Director. He did not care about my stuttering, which made me like him even more. I still tried to hide my stutter as best as I could. We became boyfriend and girlfriend my junior year. We went to the same church but not the same school. Neither of us had our own car at the time and we did not always have access to a car. He lived in the city, and I lived in the county, so we did not see each other much outside of church. We talked on the phone in order to keep in touch. I had a cell phone, but he did not. This meant I would have to call his house phone, and he lived with three brothers, one sister, his mom and stepdad. For fluent speakers, there would not be a second thought given to just calling and asking for him. But for me, it caused incredible anxiety. I did not know who would answer the phone, and when they answered, I did not know if I would be able to get out, "Hi, is JJ home?" On top of that, I did not know if they would ask, "Who is calling?" which would require me to say my name, which begins with a hard letter that would cause me to stutter more often than not.

So much thought went into one little phone call that during the conversation the night before JJ and I would hang up, we would discuss who would call whom the next day. If he was to call me, I made sure to keep my cell phone next to me so that I would not miss his call and have to call him back and go through the agonizing struggle of making that call. If I was to call him, I made sure to let him know exactly when I would be calling so that he would answer and no one else. I knew there was a possibility that someone might be on the phone when it was time for me to call and they would have to click over to take my call, so I was always on edge whenever I dialed that number. From what I remember, I never actually had the problem of having to speak to members of JJ's family. Thank goodness! Just in case, I would practice saying my name, I would practice saying, "Hi, is JJ home?" and I would hum and do my best to relax my vocal chords so I could keep the stuttering to a minimum. Dealing with these phone calls offers just a taste of the struggle of dating with a stutter; there are more tales of struggles to come.

During the years I was in high school, Facebook became a pretty huge deal. This was back when you had to be invited to be on the site, so it was exclusive and everyone wanted to be on it. This was also the time when I started realizing how small St. Louis really was. All of a sudden there was quick, easy access to talk to people you thought were cute and attractive. For a stutterer, this was golden. I could meet someone without being embarrassed by my stuttering. They could get to know me, and we could communicate without my feeling pressured to hurry up and talk or feel pressured to hide how I talk. I could show the real me and hold real conversations without worrying about my stuttering's being a barrier and demanding attention like the Great Wall of China.

Because of this sort of physical barrier in my life, I never really had long, intellectual conversations. With my condition, I always felt I was holding everyone up and wasting their time and wondered if people even understood what I was saying because I was pausing so often. I was not on the receiving end of my impediment, so I did not know if people would be able to piece together what I was saying in between all the pauses. That is why, to this day, I repeat things or word my sentences in a repetitive way because I fear that some people do not understand me. In my mid-20s I dated a guy named CJ who brought that fear to life. In doing so, he made me realize he was not "the one," even though he promised to marry me during our time together.

CJ and I were very goal-focused, and we often talked about business and financial activities. Since I was working as a benefits administrator, I was able to educate him on retirement planning and different avenues to go about securing his future, such as a 401(k), IRAs, and how to increase the value on investments through compound interest.

One night we were on the phone talking about financial investments and the like, I was stuttering pretty badly. Midway through the conversation, he interrupted me and told me he could not understand what I was saying because his attention was bad. He said he always had a hard time focusing and all the pausing in my stuttering made it hard for him to focus on what I was saying. Hearing this, I was offended. I was hurt. This guy I loved was telling me he could not focus long enough to understand me with my stutter. As usual I tended to blame myself—my stuttering—not him for being a jerk. In an effort to atone for the inconvenience I had caused him by my speech, I told him I would just write an email detailing everything I was trying to say. The next day, after he read the email, he asked me if I had copied and pasted the contents from somewhere because it was so intelligent, detailed, and technical. I did not think about it then, the implicit criticism; I took it as a compliment. Now, though, I look back on it and realize the person I was dating could not see the full range of my mental ability until I wrote, because my stuttering had dumbed me down, to put it bluntly.

The matter with CJ was an isolated incident, thank God, and it came years after I had already convinced myself of the contradiction between my spoken and written thoughts. Because I always felt I could write better than I talked, I never really participated in deep conversations or heated debates about politics or music, or really anything. I felt I was always slowing down the conversation. As a matter of fact, to this day, I do not communicate with spoken words as well on serious issues as I would like to. Stuttering aside and just focusing on the content of my words, I feel as though I do not speak as eloquently and intelligently as I do when I write, because I do not formulate the best way to say things in conversation as quickly as other people do, simply because I have never had to.

Facebook allowed an outlet for me to talk to guys, but also to express myself and showcase my mind and not the stutter that preceded my mind. My status updates always drew comments from people. My Aunt Deborah once told me that she read my status, and I always spoke so wisely. My dad called me diplomatic. Facebook allowed me the opportunity to talk. *Finally.* I always said that if I could talk as well as I write, I would be further ahead in life. I am sure, reading that, my dad would say or think that that alone should be motivation enough for me to want to work on my stuttering. But my lack of patience for the process hinders that inspiration.

Anyway, for this shy, reserved girl, Facebook brought my first love, DJ, the summer after I graduated from high school. I do not even remember accepting his friend request, but I did. He said he was drawn to my profile picture and had to find out who this "chocolate girl" was. We talked a little through Facebook, but soon after our conversation began there, he wanted to talk on the phone. I did not have too long of an opportunity to speak to him before my stuttering spoke for me.

Before DJ and I spoke on the phone, I told him I stuttered. I broke down that my stuttering was more like long pauses than it was the exaggerated Hollywood style of stuttering—stammering and repeating words or parts of words. He did not mind. He worked the front desk at a high-rise apartment complex for the affluent, and he said he would call me from there in his downtime.

I remember our first conversation, and he asked me how to pronounce my name. We talked about a few small things; he ended that he was happy to finally have heard my voice. *Interesting.* For me the focus was on my stutter. For him the focus was the voice behind the stutter.

We had a couple of more conversations on the phone before he invited me with his family to Six Flags. I was nervous about our first date being surrounded by people as opposed to one on one. In every social situation, my stuttering is the first thing I think about as I try to protect myself from embarrassment and awkwardness. First dates were stressful enough for me; meeting family at the same time added a whole extra level of struggle. In the words of Kevin Hart, "I was not ready!"

If I am comfortable with a person, then I do not mind going out in groups with others I do not know. I usually talk to the person beforehand and let them know to introduce me or let them know these situations make me nervous. That way it helps alleviate the stress and tension, which always make my stuttering worse. It also makes me feel I have an ally so that if a situation comes up where I start stuttering badly, I know that person will have my back. When I go out alone with people I rarely talk to or am not comfortable with and we are around other people who have no idea I stutter, I feel the way I did in school when I was about to give a speech in front of a class. Anything I say, if I stutter, I feel will put me on display.

All of these internal conversations went on even before I reached DJ and his family, so my sensitivity to my stuttering was heightened. As I sat at the entrance waiting for them to arrive, I was nervous. As everyone walked up, I realized no one was even thinking about me except DJ. His little brother decided to stick with us, but everyone else went off on their own. My fears, thank heavens, were baseless. I had spent days worrying only to find out the worst was just a figment of my imagination—not that I was complaining.

The rest of the date went well, other than the fact that I starved myself because I was so self-conscious about eating in front of DJ. When I finally broke down and let him order me some food, I smashed those hot wings so fast that he talks about it to this day if you bring up our first date at Six Flags.

I was not really feeling DJ after the date, because I thought he had been a showoff for asking me to hold his money. It seemed as if it was payday because it was easily one thousand dollars. Who needs that at a theme park? A showoff, that's who! So, I was nice, and we parted ways. Later that night, I realized I had his ID still in my purse. Just my luck. I was hoping not to have to see him again. Not because he had done anything wrong, but because I did not want him to try to change my mind about giving him a second chance. I returned his ID and that is exactly what ended up happening. By the end of the summer, we had fallen in love and were a couple.

Back then, early in our relationship, DJ was still working the night shift at the high-rise. Since it was summer, and I had no classes or a job, I spent time with him whenever I could. I would take dinner to his job sometimes, and we would just talk in the lobby. One night, DJ wanted dinner but neither of us had brought anything to eat. Since he was on the clock, he could not leave, but he wanted me to make a McDonald's run. For fluent-speakers, you would not think twice: It would be a quick run to Mickey D's and back. But as soon as he asked if I would go grab him the food, my thought was I would have to order from the drive-thru because the main restaurant was closed. For me, a drive-thru was right up there with making cold calls. The person cannot see you and all focus is on your voice. They cannot tell that you are stuck trying to get a word out. I told DJ I really did not like the drive-thru because of the anxiety it caused me with the pressure of trying to order without embarrassing myself and stuttering too badly. But he really wanted it, so I gave in. When you are in love, sometimes fear does not reign supreme. Real love makes you feel you can do anything. I went to McDonald's and ordered. I cannot remember the extent of my stuttering, but I know I spoke clearly enough to bring him back his dinner so I must not have stuttered too badly. I do remember thinking he had not made a big deal out of it, especially not as big of a deal as I had made. Interestingly, the next night he told me he had called his best friend and told him I went through the drive-thru for him. It is the simple things: A love like . . . going through the drive-thru. I will never forget how proud of me he was, with the biggest grin on his face, as he gave me the most heartfelt hug. That was the beginning.

As time went on and we got more comfortable with each other, we talked about my stuttering and he expressed desire to help me improve. We used to lie in bed and listen to YouTube, one of our ways to just vibe out. We would talk about everything and nothing, and he would have me repeat sentences back to him. Of all the guys I have dated since then and of all the ways I have tried to convince myself it was real with someone else, this simple game we played created the safest space for me to be myself and better myself. The thing I tried to hide from guys, and people in general, DJ was trying to help me with. I did not want the help in middle school or high school; it was love that helped me open up to others, helping me to help myself. The thing that matters the most to us always teaches us the most valuable lessons. Love matters most and love helped my stutter.

Soon, our summer romance, filled with free time and good times, was replaced with classes and homework, as college was soon to begin. Upon completing high school, I met all the requirements necessary to receive the benefits offered through the A+ program. This program was offered to high school students, who, upon meeting the community service, grade-point-average, and attendance thresholds, would be awarded two free years of community college. Most students used these first two years to get their prerequisites out of the way before transferring to a four-year university, which is exactly what I did. One of the first classes I took, only because it was required, was oral communications. I wanted to get it out the way and not stress about it in the upcoming semesters. As I had done throughout high school, I used my IEP with my professors to avoid talking aloud.

In truth, I used the IEP as a crutch. Initially, I did not want to have an IEP because I knew that once I graduated from college the real world would not have an "IEP" to "save" me. My mom, being the mother hen she was (and still is!), suggested I get one just in case. So, I did. It did not matter much in my oral communication class though because instead of the break or special treatment I received in middle school and high school, I got no preferential treatment in college. The teacher introduced me on the first day and told everyone I stuttered and that they should be patient and make me feel comfortable, but made it clear I was going to be presenting and giving speeches just like the rest of the class. As grown as I wanted to feel, I did not think I was ready to be an adult. Knowing that I would not get out of talking in front of the class freaked me out. We had to give four to five presentations during the semester. All but one of them were solo. It was easy to hide during group presentations because I could always get away with saying one small portion and letting everyone else take the reins. But I was beyond terrified at the thought of flying solo.

Surprisingly, I do not remember the first few presentations of the semester. I know they were all timed and the only preferential treatment I was given was a few extra minutes. For everyone else, the teacher deducted points from their score if they were over or under time, but even though she gave me more time to give my presentation, she never considered that as a factor when grading.

All throughout that class, my concern was never the content of my speeches, but always the delivery. Many people think stuttering affects my mental abilities, but confidence in my intellect has never been a concern. Fluent speakers tend to care more about content, and that was the least of my worries, if a worry at all. Years of stuttering had made me quiet, so I cultivated my writing. My confidence in written communication far exceeded my confidence in verbal communication. So, it was never about how good the speech was that I was giving, but always about how my actual speech and speaking were.

The last speech in that class is what really stood out to me. I volunteered to go first and get the speech out of the way since it would be the last one we would have to give for the class. I just wanted it over with. It was a solo speech and was not timed. We had to discuss research we had done. Again, I was not worried about the content because I knew that would always be good enough, so I do not remember the topic of my research. Conversely, I remember the day clearly.

That morning I woke up trying to calm my nerves, knowing my presentation was on the horizon. I tried to be as Zen as possible and hum out any tension in my throat. That was a relaxation technique I tended to do before I had any speaking engagement. I wanted my vocal chords to be as relaxed as possible, and I knew from experience that the more I exercised them, the less I stuttered. I came to that realization from working out. After a good session at the gym, complete with heavy breathing, my entire body, including my throat, always seemed more open and at ease. The result: I stuttered less. Humming was a verbal gymnastics, of sorts, for my throat. That particular day, I tried to ease out the tension and relax the muscles so I would be loose and ready at the time of the speech.

As soon as I entered the class, adrenaline kicked in and all that relaxation preparation went completely out the window. I tried to calm my nerves by telling myself my classmates had all seen me give presentations before so this would not be a surprise to anyone. I tried to tell myself that no one would laugh. I tried to tell myself everything was OK.

My time came to give the speech, and I walked up to the podium. I prefer to give presentations behind something that covers the majority of my body because of the tics and tricks I use to get the words out. This podium hid nothing, which meant I had to keep the movements to a minimum so as not to embarrass myself further. Having to restrict my movements and maintain my composure due to not having a podium caused me to stutter more, or in my mind these tricks were necessary so I stuttered more as a result of this subconscious reasoning. Either way, I was behind this podium that might as well have not been there because it was as thin as a toothpick.

The entire room was silent, and I felt the pressure of no less than thirty sets of eyes burning into me. I started off relatively smoothly, as smoothly as a stutterer can be. And then it happened: I hit my first few blocks and realized the deafening silence as I was trying to get the words out. I became hyper-aware of my stuttering and more self-conscious than ever. The more I started to stress about my stuttering in front of everyone, the worse it became. I started sweating, but I did not wipe my face because I thought it would make my nerves noticeable. I hoped the class could not see the sweat to the extent that I could feel it. I started getting the urge to tap harder to get the words out, but I could not because the toothpick podium would give it away. By now, I had started shaking slightly, a mix of frustration and not getting the words out. In the middle of the speech, I became so upset that my eyes started watering. I did not want to break down in front of the class, so I held my tears back.

For some 10 seemingly endless minutes, I stood giving this speech. When it was finally over I felt nothing but relief that I would not have to give another presentation ever again. To this day, I have not. Throughout the rest of my education, including my master's program, I was exempted from giving presentations. In my oral communications class I was still not out of the woods with my speech, as the class would now analyze my presentation. Sitting at my desk, I braced myself as a student began his critique. He let me know that however well I had thought I was hiding my emotions during the speech, I was not at all. He said I had started off well, but then I began getting frustrated and he could tell. He said the more frustrated I got, the harder it was for me to speak. But then he said there had been no need for me to get frustrated because my presentation was really good. Before I knew it, several other classmates had echoed his sentiments. To add to my relief, the teacher agreed with all of them. Thus, while they were critiquing my presentation, I finally let out the tears I had been holding in from the beginning.

For so long, I had been so hard on myself. I felt as though I were a failure because my stuttering was seemingly so bad that I convinced myself no one could understand me. To hear those words of encouragement and positivity was almost more than I could bear, as my tears had demonstrated. I once heard a quote that said, "Never believe them when they say you are great, because you will believe them when they say you are not." While it is true that the opinions and thoughts we have of ourselves should always mean more than those of others, sometimes it is necessary to have reminders that we are OK.

Negative self-talk can hold us back, and, in the case of my stuttering, I feel has held me back at times. If I had never had others assuring me that I was doing well even when I thought I was not, I would still think that no one could understand me.

Even when I attempt to use Siri and/or record a text message into my phone, the software fails to register my words and basically says, "Huh?" or the message comes out as gibberish as though I'd had a stroke in the process of saying, "Good morning! How are you?" So, while it is necessary and very obvious that I need to improve my self-confidence about my speaking ability, it is good to hear that where I am now is OK. In that moment after my speech, I needed that reassurance. As embarrassed as I was to cry in a college class where I was supposed to be grown and was surrounded by other adults, I was happy to be finished and know that not only was the content of my speech good enough, but the delivery of the speech, even with my stuttering, was fine the way it was.

The rest of community college was a breeze, other than some headwinds in Spanish 1 and Spanish 2. I can barely talk in English, so imagine trying to have folks understand me in another language. That struggle "speaks" for itself.

So, what about DJ? Well, all throughout my time at community college, DJ and I dated. The plan in my mind was always to transfer to an art college and major in fashion design, ideally in Chicago. DJ begged me not to leave him, and my father told me an art degree and a nickel would get me a cup of coffee. I ended up taking their advice, as they were influential in my life at that time, and decided in favor of DJ and against design school. I have always been the kind of woman who wanted to please the men in her life, sometimes more than I wanted to please myself. So, instead of going to design school in Chicago, I stayed and finished my bachelors at the University of Missouri-St. Louis (UMSL).

If I had to give one reason why the majority of my twenties has been full of both hope and heartbreak, that need to please those outside of myself is why. I was about twenty-eight when I finally decided to disregard what others said about me and love myself first. This new way of seeing myself was thrillingly liberating.

After nearly two years of being together and right before I transferred to UMSL, DJ and I had an amicable breakup. Soon after, I met an African who changed my life. Not necessarily for the better, and not necessarily for the worse . . .

EJ was a student at the community college, but I did not notice him much at all because I was in a relationship with DJ most of that time. I did see him, though. He caught my eye because I love chocolate, dark skin. Even so, I never initiated contact with him because no matter how young I was, I was old-school and believed a man should approach the woman, and because my stuttering would have made for an awkward introduction. Imagine walking up to someone and trying to get a word out but you are so nervous you are stuck. You are just standing there not saying anything, making a face trying to get the words out to pierce the painful silence. Reason enough as to why I never approached anyone in person. That explains, I like to joke, why God invented Facebook. I found EJ on Facebook somehow—I did not even know his name at the time, but I have always been a good detective when it comes to finding things and making connections on social media. Like any good sleuth, I was not all that surprised that I found him. Not much gets past me, including EJ. We did not actually start talking, though, until I transferred to UMSL.

I remember one of our first conversations because he cracked the corniest joke. We were texting, so he had not heard me stutter—*yet*. I told him I stuttered so that when we eventually did talk in person or on the phone, he would not be surprised. It never occurred to me that he was conscious of his own speech as well. He said something to the effect of, "We both are having a hard time with English because I am African and you stutter." I laughed so hard. Therein began my love for Africans that would grow so deep that my friends would jokingly call me racist because Africans were the only guys that approached me and I dated for years. Even to this day, I am approached by more African men than I am African-American men.

EJ and I would go on to date on and off for several years, and even if our relationship did not last, I have his speaking English joke to thank for igniting my love for Africans.

Now that I was at a university with more people and opportunities, I was dating more. Dating with a stutter is definitely interesting to say the least. I came across numerous guys who liked my stuttering. Some called it cute, like a guy who was waiting for me to get "lettuce" out when I was ordering at Subway. I have never quite seen the cuteness in it, especially when I am trying to get a word out and my face scrunches up into a lookalike of Chewbacca. Nonetheless, cute is the top description I have gotten from men when they talk about my stuttering. Another guy I dated (he was African as well) took a cue from the singer Trey Songz and called the faces I make when I stutter "love faces." To this I aptly replied that the faces were more like Chewbacca. But this guy liked me, so, of course, he did not agree with my comparison.

Then there were those guys who let their pride get in the way and decided to handle my stuttering as though it were their feelings that were hurt and to heck with decency and respect. Take, for example, a man (I use the term here loosely) I met at a gas station. He came up to me and wanted my number. He was not too terrible looking, so I decided to oblige him and hand over my digits. We talked on the phone a couple of times to set up a date, and he knew from meeting me that I stuttered. He had no issue with it. He had nothing but a big, toothy smile from the time we crossed paths at the gas station to the time we ended up on our first date at Applebee's. The date really was not memorable and from what I do remember, he kept trying to stare down my shirt the entire time. Anyone who knows me knows I love to show skin, but I keep it classy. Besides, I am skinny with itty bitties, so there was not much for him to stare at in the first place. Needless to say, I was turned off, but I waited until the date was over and the next day had come. I texted him that I was not really interested, but in a very diplomatic way. Apparently, I was a wrecking ball to his fragile ego because his response was, "That's OK. We would not have worked out anyway because you cannot talk." I laughed. Hard. The poor man could not handle rejection. But he was not even the worst, not by a long shot.

In graduate school I was approached by a guy who lived in the same apartment complex in which I lived. We met on the bus. In Chicago everyone rides the bus. Parking and traffic are the worst, and you would be doing yourself a favor to catch a ride. But I digress. So, I was leaving school; he was leaving work. We got off at the same stop, and he went his way toward his building, but not before talking to me and getting my number. He was in his late 20s/early 30s, so his approach was different. There was not a bunch of texting and "wyd (what are you doing)" me to death. He simply called and asked me out, and we went out for dinner. He knew I stuttered. He also had a friend who stuttered, which made him Captain Stutter Expert. He was also a first-generation Nigerian-American. He told me his father lived in Nigeria and that, because of their Islamic faith, his father had many wives. My date was one of twenty-some-odd children fathered by one man, birthed by at least five wives! This is important, for it can be the only justification for his talking out the side of his neck as if he had ownership over me and my speech. As we sat at dinner and ordered our meal, he became even more intrigued by my stuttering. He went on to tell me how he had helped his friend improve his speech and he wanted to help me, too. I did not ask for his help, but that did not stop him from telling me to "slooow down," emphasizing the words in an effort to show me what he meant. He wanted me to follow his lead and do what he said. Again, I did not ask for help. After so many instances of his telling me to slow down and telling me how I would improve my speech if I just used this or that technique, it finally dawned on him that I was ignoring his unsolicited help. Captain Stutter Expert got so fed up that he told me to be quiet, using those exact words. "Just be quiet," he said.

Anyone who knows me knows I do not do well with orders and demands from anyone who is not in a position to actually exercise authority over me. Which is basically anyone other than the elders in my family, my parents, and God. So, this individual, whom I knew just long enough to snap a finger, clearly was not on my list of authority figures. But being that no one had ever been so unambiguously rude to me, I was shocked. Honestly, I do not remember too much about my reaction, other than that I was disappointed in my *lack* of reaction. I do not even want to give myself the excuse that I was young, because I did not hold my tongue when people close to me spoke out of turn. I do not want to give myself the excuse that I was new to the city and did not really know my way around enough to get back home, because I had unlimited data and could have figured it out just as I figured how to get to school, home, and everywhere else in Chicago. There was no excuse for my silence other than that I tend to tolerate more from men because of this sense of trying to please them instead of speaking up for myself, just as I had done with my ex, DJ, and with my dad by not going to design school. I am this hopeless romantic and I do not usually take my mind with me whenever my heart goes on a cloud-nine adventure. That is how I ended up with CJ and his tomfoolery about how he loved me but cut me off mid-sentence saying he could not pay attention and follow what

I was saying because of the pauses. To further demonstrate the pattern of behavior, that is how I ended up in a seven-year, on-and-off relationship with EJ. This pattern was also on display that night with Captain Stutter Expert. Even though in that moment I did not speak up to him (I also did not stay quiet as he demanded, either), he did not get another chance to talk to me after that night. My silence those times he reached out after that night spoke loudly enough. Even still, this situation was not even the worst.

CHAPTER FIVE

The Battle: Stutter vs Job

In 2011, I graduated from college and made a spur-of-the-moment decision to move to Rockford to live with my dad, stepmom, and younger siblings. By this time, Celene and Tyson were not so young anymore. Celene was eleven and Tyson was nine. I was twenty-two. Wade had already gotten married and was stationed in Texas in the Air Force. Being the oldest sibling in closest proximity to my little brother and sister, and therefore the one who was looked to as an example on a daily basis, I felt an immense pressure to make something of myself, and to do it rather quickly. I had not taken the GMAT or applied to any graduate schools, and I did not have a job. Within the first few weeks of moving in with my dad, I hurried to take the GMAT and apply to graduate schools before the application deadlines arrived. I did not study for the test but still got into graduate school. I know I did terribly on the math section (surprising after I majored in accounting and went on to get my degree in accounting in graduate school as well), but the writing section saved me from an epic fail as I scored in the top 5th percentile. I was not surprised by that. Remember, my silence in speech has allowed me to become a force to be reckoned with in written communication.

I got accepted to a few schools in Chicago, but ultimately, I chose to go to the University of Illinois at Chicago. Once I settled on a school, it was time for me to settle on an apartment. Because I was with my dad now, I knew that I would be in charge of all communication when it came to apartment hunting. I would have to schedule all the apartment tours and reach out on my own with any questions I had. Thankfully, I was born in the internet age, so those parts were not too stressful for me. I was able to schedule all the apartment tours online through email and the companies' websites. Sometimes the companies would call to confirm my appointment, but talking was easier when I was not the one initiating a phone call, as answering the phone released the pressure of having to call and immediately speak. So, I could handle that. At the apartment tours, again, my dad took a backseat and I drove the communication the entire appointment. Of course, he asked questions that I would not think to ask as a first-time apartment hunter, but he did not step in at any time to speak for me or fill in awkward silences as my mom would have done.

Eventually, I found an apartment I liked and that satisfied my bougie standards. About a week before school started, with help from my pops, Celene, and Tyson, I moved in. When I say "help," I mean they all helped me bring everything up to my apartment and put it all on the floor. My dad helped me put my bed frame together then he and my siblings immediately left. I was used to my mom, who would have helped me unpack everything, set up the kitchen, hang my bathroom towels all cute, the works. But my dad was a guy through and through. He did the heavy lifting (literally) and the rest was on me. Plus, Tyson had a baseball game to attend, and his kids' sports and extracurricular activities were always top priority for Dad. He almost skipped my high-school graduation because Celene had a prior Girl Scout commitment. And for my graduate-school graduation, Celene had to leave early for a volleyball game. So, when I say sports and extracurricular activities were a top priority, I am not exaggerating. I joke with my family that no one dare die on the day of a championship game or something similarly important. Try to hold the last breath until the game is over, at least, because it is a possibility family just might not make it. I may be exaggerating a bit when it comes to the death part, but everything else is fair game.

I was not too nervous about navigating my new life on my own and steering my way around Chicago. As long as I did not have to speak or talk, I was never really nervous about much else. The things most people fear from being in a new city—being alone, figuring out how to get around—those things were never a concern for me. I think that is why God gave me a stutter and one of the reasons that it has never gone away. Stuttering is my only real insecurity. I have said for years that it is what keeps me humble; it is what keeps me from getting ahead of myself and slows me down, literally and figuratively. The decision to go to grad school, while inevitable, was still very spur of the moment and did not take much thought. I have a habit of moving fast in life, and my stuttering, while sometimes functioning as an anchor, has never kept me from acting decisively when the situation called for it.

I was not anchored when I moved to Chicago. I went out to the beach the weekend before class started. The first man I ran into was a guy named RJ. He was young—twenty—and he kept hitting on me, but I did not pay him the slightest attention. Plus, he was short, and as I have mentioned, I did not date people who were shorter than I was. He decided to put his beach towel right by me, and he was loud talking about how beautiful I was, everyone within earshot laughing at his boldness. So, I was like, "OK, just sit!" if only to get him to quit being so loud. We ended up talking about how I had just moved to town to start my master's in accounting, which led us to talking about money and finances. I did not really think he was listening; I thought he was just trying to be smooth.

Fast forward six years. I had not been in touch with him since that day at the beach. I do not even remember giving him my number, but obviously I did, as, one morning, I received a text that said, "I remember a conversation we had about saving money and staying at home. Do you remember? You influenced me. I am twenty-six and just purchased my first house. Thanks to you and how you told me to go about it." Then he ended the conversation with, "Thanks for being that beautiful girl at the beach with the brains." It was RJ. I remember trying to hide my stuttering from him, even though dating him was of no interest to me. For him to reach out and remember me for my mind and not my stuttering was extremely meaningful. Again, the boulder of an issue I thought my stuttering to be, was only a pebble to many others.

The first day of graduate school arrived and, as with all my first days of school, I had the jitters. I went to my classes way ahead of time in order to meet the teachers and beat the other students, just as I had always done. The difference in graduate school was I felt I was grown—I was no longer dragging around an IEP. Still, I felt almost child-like for choosing to explain to the teachers that I stuttered and preferred not to speak aloud. No matter how grown I was, and felt, I still was not disposed to put my stuttering on display in front of a large group. So, I let my situation be known up front to ease my nerves and prevent any potential embarrassment.

Being in graduate school meant I was well aware of the impending finality of my academic journey. A doctoral program was not in my plans, although I did consider going to law school for a millisecond. I knew that after this stint in grad school, the end would come. I would have to get a job. So, I started making plans for the future.

Trying to find a job and also going through grad school in a different city and state, and pretty much alone, was definitely a challenge. Never really the outgoing type because of my stuttering, I was trying to navigate my way solo. I remember numerous times feeling alone and sometimes flirting with tears about it. Luckily, one of my brother's close college friends, Andre, lived in Chicago, and I met up with him at a bar with a bunch of his friends in what was my introduction to Chicago nightlife and socializing.

That night, I met three of Andre's friends, whom we will simply call The Crew—and thus began a year of kicking it hard with the four of them. The Crew was even our name on GroupMe, and, oh, what crazy GroupMe conversations we had.

Other than grad school and The Crew, my main memories of Chicago were the job searches and interviews I went on. Even so, I grew pretty close with one member of The Crew, TJ, whom, for a moment, I started to like. We went on a date or two, but eventually we both came to our senses and realized it was not going to work. It took all of about two or three weeks to realize that. Soon after we drifted apart, he decided to take to Twitter to talk about me. Things I had shared with him in confidence, such as not being able to get a job because I stuttered, he now chose to share publicly. At one point, he said, "I have to get ready to go to work tomorrow, something you know nothing about." Looking back on it, I should not have cared because knowing that I shared something personal with him; which he then used it to attack me showed a defect in his character, not mine. But, I admit, it did sting. Had it been a random person, I would have felt nothing, but to have someone you had a level of trust with use your insecurity against you, that hurt. But as Beyoncé said, "Always stay gracious; best revenge is your paper." Now I go on international trips twice a year thanks to the pay from my job, something he knows nothing about!

But this job and the security it offers did not come without much heartache, doubt, tears, and hopelessness. My job hunt began in grad school. I scoured Monster.com and Craigslist for jobs though, at least initially, I did not even try to apply for corporate openings because I never thought I would be able to make it into a larger company. I counted myself out before the recruiters and hiring managers ever could—a defense mechanism for self-preservation. I once had a meeting with a job recruiter, with whom I did not inform up front that I stuttered. When I sat down to talk to him, he was caught off guard and a bit wide-eyed at my stuttering. His initial response to my stuttering was, "You know, some of the clients I work with are going to think you have mental disabilities because you stutter. Does stuttering affect your mental capacity?" After that meeting, I followed up with him a few times to see if he had any job leads, but I got the hint rather quickly that he was not interested in placing me in a job. I could tell he did not want to risk making himself look bad, due to his negative assumptions about my stuttering.

Eventually, instead of going through recruiters and big-name companies, I applied to smaller companies which maybe did not have standards as high as corporate America. These were companies where I knew I had a chance at being hired. I interviewed at small accounting firms of maybe four or five people, firms that were looking for an accounts receivable or accounts payable clerk.

Then one day during a break from working on a group project with my classmates, the African student we were working with told us that she had secured a job at a Fortune 500 company right out of graduate school making $60,000 a year. At the time, $60,000 was something I thought would be attainable only in my dreams. Hearing a fellow black woman say that made me think I could infiltrate corporate America, too.

I applied to larger, Top 100 accounting firms and Fortune 500 companies. I got interviews. Much to my surprise, I got a lot of interviews. I came to realize that what I had sold myself short on was actually well within my skill and knowledge range, though it also drove home the dispiriting realization that it was my stuttering (and not my character or my intellect) that kept me from getting hired. Ford Motor Company, Enterprise, and Boeing were just a few of the more than 40 companies I had interviews with starting with my graduation from college in 2011.

The most nerve-racking interview had to be the one with Boeing. I was accustomed to being in interviews with one or two other people, but the Boeing interview had five sets of eyes staring back at me. It was at a big table with the interviewers' seats pushed close to each other, and then mine, opposite all of them. It was all-too-similar to my dreaded school presentations. All the preparation to relax my throat and speech that I went through for the interview went out the window the moment I opened my mouth. I could answer their questions with ease, but just as with the presentations in my oral communications class in undergrad, I was tied in knots about the delivery.

Unfortunately, it seemed every interviewer was only concerned with my delivery as well. I did not get a job offer at Boeing. I walked out of most interviews knowing I would not get the job. Although sometimes the interviewers gave me hope and I truly believed I would get a call back or a job offer, but that turned out not to be the case for two long years.

I continued to interview, I continued to try. My stepmom's niece told me that I had a lot of courage to keep trying. But I thought, "What's the alternative?" I could live with my parents for the rest of my life and leech off of them, but I was fully capable of supporting myself so that was never a viable option. I admit I did think I would never get a job, and those negative thoughts took a toll on my spirit.

Nothing quite took its toll on me like an interview I had for a position at the same school where I earned my master's degree. After graduation, I remained in Chicago for a few months until my lease was up at my apartment. This gave me the opportunity to pursue more interviews in the city I had come to love. The summer after graduation, I heard about an accounting position at UIC through the school's job-listing website. It was in a department I had never been in while I attended the university. I figured the fact that I was a graduate of the school would help me secure the job and that the people would be less likely to hold my stuttering against me since they knew the high standards of the school, and that I had graduated with and benefitted from those same high standards.

I showed up early to the interview so that I would not have to rush and figure out where the department was located and the interview would be taking place. I wanted to be able to catch my breath, relax, and practice my breathing so that by the time I got to the interview I would be relatively fluent. About twenty minutes later it was time for the interview, whereby two faculty members interviewed me for the position. I had never seen them before, but no student knows every member of their university so I was not worried. I stuttered in the interview, per usual. There was one man who mainly listened and one who asked questions. I could tell the questioner had dismissed me for the position even before he told me. And he did, in fact, tell me. For the first time, an interviewer confirmed what I already knew, yet was never told because it is indeed illegal to discriminate for a position based on a disability when, if reasonable accommodations can be made, the job could be performed as well as anyone else would be able to.

I do not know if it was ignorance of the law by this individual, but what he told me next has stayed with me ever since. Stopping the interview, he said, "I am going to be honest with you. I do not want you to leave here and think you got the job. I do not want to get your hopes up and disappoint you. I am not going to offer you the job because of your speech. Hiring you with your stutter would be like throwing you into the lion's den, and the people you would be communicating with would chew you up."

In his heart of hearts, I truly believe he thought he was doing the right thing. He thought he was doing me a favor. Tears welled up in my eyes as he said that. I felt deflated and dispirited. This university, where I had just spent a year studying and working hard, paying thousands of dollars, essentially told me they would take my money, but they would not employ me. I was hurt. It was not so much the interviewer who hurt me, but what he represented: systemic unfairness. I was not naïve or oblivious to the way the real world worked, but to hear it and have it confirmed added a weight I was not quite ready to bear. I did not let the tears fall in the interview. I did not let him see me cry. The moment I stepped out of his office and into the hallway, I broke down. I cried walking to the bus stop. I cried while I waited on the corner for my bus to come. I cried the entire bus ride home. By the time I got to my apartment, I was drained. I went to bed. When I woke up, I replayed the conversation. To this day, that is the worst stuttering outcome I have had, and most assuredly, the one I will never forget.

Because I was still not working, and having finished graduate school, I moved out of my apartment and left Chicago in August 2012. I moved back in with my dad; it seemed as though nothing had changed in my life except that now I had a paper telling me I had a master's degree—and the loan debt to drive it home.

A couple of weeks after returning home, I received an email from the HR recruiter/manager for UIC telling me about an accounting position that had come open. Once I dug into the listing, I realized it was the exact same position I had been denied by the man who wanted to "save me from the lion's den." I told the HR recruiter/manager the situation and what was said in the first interview. I did not hear from her again, but I did receive a second interview. Prior to going to the second interview, I thought there had been a change of heart and that I potentially had a chance to get the job after all.

Since I was back at my dad's house now, I had to drive to the train station, take the train to Chicago, and catch the bus to UIC, a 90-minute journey all told. Wearing my suit in the summertime heat, I walked to the same building where I had my first interview. I arrived early (as usual), apprehensive about what awaited. I quickly realized the tone of this interview was different. Again, I had two interviewers. But this time I could tell they were there to appease me, not hire me. Their questions and demeanor were apathetic in regard to my responses to their questions. One man asked a few questions. He just went down the list but had no follow-up questions. Another man, who arrived late, did no more than listen. When the first man asked the other man if he had anything else to ask me, the two looked at each other, clearly just going through the motions. It became crystal clear they were never going to offer me the job. It was not even a consideration. The only genuine gesture came from the HR manager's initially reaching out about the opening. From that point on the university was just trying to save face. I will always wonder what conversation was held sub rosa between the man from the first interview and the interviewers from the second interview. When I got back to my dad's house, I realized, and we both agreed, the university had no intention of doing anything with the second interview other than build a case in their favor to head me off if I tried to take legal action against their discriminatory practices.

That and other disappointments aside, I had to keep pushing. It was not for nothing that the word "Resilient" was tattooed on my ribs. The pain in getting that tattoo was symbolic in and of itself. I bounced back from the failed interviews—always have, always will. I started thinking seriously about joining either the military or the Peace Corps. I figured the military would be an easy in, but I also knew that it would be a lifetime commitment. I cannot even commit to keeping my hair in one style for more than two weeks, my hairdo being the equivalent of having my own child, so I was pretty sure I did not want to join the military and left that as a last-resort option.

Instead, I started the process for the Peace Corps. A friend of mine from Chicago had recently left for Ethiopia as a Peace Corps volunteer. I had always wanted to go to Africa, so I was very excited about the Peace Corps. I completed the application, had an interview and was waiting for the acceptance and geographical assignment when I got word that I had been awarded an unpaid internship in St. Louis. My master's in accounting in hand and my interviews with all those big-name companies to the contrary notwithstanding, the best job offer I could get was an unpaid accounting internship for a tiny non-profit, run out of the executive director's home.

"Chastened" does not do my state of mind justice, but I had to humble myself. I was frustrated that this job was the best I could do, but I stayed calm. Quietly, I transitioned, making the move back to St. Louis. Letting my pride go, I worked for free (at least I was able to negotiate a weekly gas allowance), and I accomplished my goal of adding more work experience to my résumé. Not many people knew I was back in St. Louis, and I preferred it that way, partly because I had just graduated and was not where I wanted to be financially and partly because I was never big on the social scene, both reasons due to my stuttering.

My internship was with EarthDance, an organic-farm school, and lasted for about three months. I was very grateful for this job and the opportunity it afforded me to gain more experience in the real world. Even though it was just an internship, it was a step up in my career, and it taught me that not all steps are vertical.

I was still waiting to hear from the Peace Corps because in my mind that was going to be my move for the next twenty-four months. Even so, I was applying and interviewing at other places and eventually decided to give myself options by talking with a military recruiter about joining the Air Force.

My dad was in the Army for years and had suggested the Air Force as the branch of choice if I were to join. My brother was in the Air Force, as well, so between those two men's advice, it seemed almost inevitable that I would choose the Air Force, too. I ended up meeting with a black woman who was an officer, a captain. We met in downtown St. Louis in her office, and I asked, and answered, a lot of questions. She appeared to be completely unfazed by my stutter. After about forty-five minutes of Q's and A's and her explaining the process, she let me know that I would have to go through a medical examination in order to join the Air Force. "No big deal," I thought. I was healthy—very healthy, in fact—working out in my free time, which I had a lot of under the circumstances. I figured if I were going to be jobless, I was at least going to work out and look good while being unemployed. I refused to be unfit *and* unemployed.

The recruiter started going into depth about the medical examination, and I thought it was weird that she would be focused on that more than anything else. Then she got to the point. She was unsure if I would pass the medical examination with my speech impediment. I had no idea what one had to do with the other, but she did not let me simmer in my ignorance for long. In case of a military emergency, she feared that my stuttering would delay communication and cause more problems than it would solve. Essentially, this was the military telling me no, too. My last-resort option ended up being no option at all. With this rejection, I really started to doubt that I would ever gain employment doing something that I would be proud of, employment that would allow me to support myself and support my motto of "Onward and Upward" in life.

My trying to find meaningful employment in St. Louis, and living back with my mom and Chuckie, meant that they were feeling my anxiety about finding a job, too. Their home was, is, and always will be a Christ-centered household, so they prayed a lot for me and my success. My momma was an ordained reverend, and every day she was doing something involving the Lord's work: preaching, teaching, volunteering, or something else in answer of the call. From time to time, she would visit other churches and encourage the family to join her. One week, a local church was having its annual revival and brought an African man as a guest speaker who was anointed with the gift of healing. As much as I loved African men, they had been the majority of my biggest headaches in the dating department, so that alone should have told me to run, not walk, in the opposite direction. I went to the service anyway. Big mistake.

The service started as would any black church service. The praise team opened up, then there were some scripture readings and prayer. The offering followed and then more singing. It was finally time for the man of the hour. He got up to preach, but right away he touted himself as more of a healer and miracle worker than a preacher. A little way into his speaking, he started "performing miracles." This is where I wondered if he could miraculously heal my stuttering. But I trusted in God's healing me before an agent of God would. He called down a woman who had menstrual issues. He said some words, placed his hands on her and told her to go to the bathroom to check and see if she had been healed. He performed some other "miracles" on people that I cannot remember. I do remember being very skeptical about the miracles he claimed he could perform and about the miracles the people were claiming he was fixing as they stood at the front of the church. Nonetheless, he kept making miracles happen and I sat there with my mom and stepdad.

At one point he said something that, to Chuckie, sounded as if he could cure my stuttering. Now my stepdad is a big guy who cares about three things: God, his family, and his money. (His food comes in a close fourth.) He will go to the ends of the earth to protect those top three. He also is very much the spontaneous type, and growing up in the hood made him a bit less reserved and conservative than my mom and me. So, when he thought the pastor might be able to cure my stuttering, he immediately jumped up and grabbed me, trying to pull me to the front of the church to get this miracle cure. I was scared Miracle Man was going to have me prove to everyone that I stuttered, and that he cured me by doing a before and after speech on the mic. I was highly uninterested in that, so when Chuckie tried to pull me up to the front, I tried to stay seated. However, when Chuckie is determined, there is no stopping him. Over my protests, I somehow ended up in the front of the church. I was anxious to the highest degree, and I was on the verge of tears. The entire humiliating experience was a blur as the man tried to perform his miracle, but I am still stuttering to this day, so . . .

When the "miracle" was over, I left. By "left", I mean I did not just leave the front and go back to my seat; I left my mom and stepdad. I left the church, and I drove home. When I got home, I closed my door and stayed to myself for the rest of the evening. My stepdad and mom tried to talk to me when they got back to the house, but I was in no mood to hear it. I kept replaying the entire series of events in my head. Was my stuttering that bad that Chuckie had to drag me down to some miracle worker? Does stuttering have that much of a negative connotation that it needed to be "healed"? Did I *want* to be healed? Did the "healing" not work because of my skepticism? So many questions, so few answers. Chuckie knew he was wrong for making me go to the front. Though Mom was not involved with Chuckie's faith move, she knew it was a mistake for Chuckie to move against my will. Both tried to engage me in conversation, but eventually they left me alone when they realized I was not interested in having a conversation. The next day Chuckie apologized. He said it was only because he cared and wanted to help.

That pretty much summed up the thinking of a lot of people in dealing with my stuttering: They wanted to help. But in "helping," they actually ended up hindering. They offered their best "It's OK" or "Take your time." But what I loved most? What made me the most appreciative? It was when a person just waited. They did not rush me or pressure me or offer up their suggestions on how I could improve a stutter that I had lived with nearly my entire life. When they just sat there, patiently, and allowed me to finish my thought, that was what I loved the most.

As a way to unwind and release tension, I started heavily attending poetry shows and open-mic nights. I would never perform, but I would slip in right before they started and slip out right as the last poet exited the stage. Spoken word is the official name of the artistry event, and even though I was not an avid poet or performer, I had always appreciated the rhythm and the passion behind each artist's piece. I have always been fascinated with how people put words together, and it always amazed me that no matter how finite the number of words there were, there was an infinite number of ways to put them together so that no poem was ever the same. I was intrigued by such poets as Corey Black and Brandon "Xplicit" Thornton, who appeared consistently on the spoken-word scene in St. Louis. But one time I went to a show and a poet named Haki Natuwah performed. I remember it exactly because the entire time he performed, he stared straight at me. You know how when you catch someone's eye you do not know, you may hold it for a second but you eventually look away? Well, neither of us looked away. He may have looked left and right a couple of times in order to keep the audience engaged, but for ninety-five percent of his poem, he stared directly at me. Not one to ever back down from a challenge, I locked eyes with him the entire poem as well. Once the poem and evening were over, everyone went their separate ways, and I ducked out as usual. Somehow Haki found me on Facebook, and we connected. I would see him at shows, and in due course he came up to speak to me, and that his how he became aware of my stutter. Eventually, I became the inspiration for one of his poems.

"Something to Say"

Words are like a small stone,
Skipping quietly along
The surface of an undisturbed lake.
But actions are like a HUGE boulder,
A confused soldier,
During a violent earthquake.
Speak and it is spoken,
Provoking small ripples in impressionable minds,
Coasting on the shores of an Ocean,
Watching souls that are hopeless lose focus in the sands of time
Standing at the edge of a cliff,
Wondering if
You have the ability to fly.

While nature boldly leaps from its nest,

Soaring high,

Or inevitably die.

You can hear a lion roar,

Volcanoes exploding,

Or thunder crack.

While the whispers of a stuttering child

Go unheard

But make the loudest and most memorable impact.

We all paid attention when OBAMA spoke and he became the

First Black President, on that unforgettable day.

But I listen patiently as that stuttering child speaks,

Because in my opinion . . .

She has something more important to say!

Inspired by: Matice Ahnjamine

Written by: Haki Natuwah

When Haki sent me this poem, he said something to me that I will always remember when I think of my stuttering. He said, "God slowed you down so others could keep up. Those who are not patient enough to listen will miss the blessing in your words." His words truly blessed me during that difficult season in my life.

I had been in St. Louis for some time at this point, about six months. I still had no paying job and had resigned myself to going with the Peace Corps once I was accepted and received my destination.

Then I received an email from a small, family-owned business called Ekon Benefits that was looking to hire someone with my educational background. While I had zero experience in the retirement plan industry, I knew numbers and that is what they wanted. I interviewed for the position; Yes, another internship, but luckily it was a paid internship. As with all my interviews, I struggled with my stuttering. But I made it through, and the interviewer said she would let me know soon what the company thought. I had hopes, but no expectations.

A few weeks went by and I had not heard back from the Ekon interview. However, I did receive a phone call to interview at a home healthcare company for which Chuckie had done some transportation for their clients. He has always been a people person and very outgoing, so he was talking to the boss and found out the company was looking for an accountant. He immediately called me while he was in the boss's office and put her on the phone. I absolutely hate cold calls, and it was hardly any better if I did not have to make the call myself but a stranger was on the other end. Nonetheless, he passed the phone and the woman on the other end asked me to email my resume within the hour. Later on, I would find out that she gave me that one-hour timeframe to see if I was actually prepared, about my business and actively looking for a job, or if I was just another person who was looking for a job but not putting in the work. With one hour to work with, that would mean I already had a resume prepared and ready to go. I did not have to take the time to create one as would someone who was not on top of her game. Made sense. What she did not know was that while I was prepared, as a stutterer I felt an obligation to work even harder in every area of business—of my *life*— just to prove I was at least equal of those who spoke fluently. Long story short: I sent the resume to her almost immediately. She emailed me to set up an interview and within a few days I was seated in her office. This was the interview where I saw that God was working on my behalf, as the purpose of the meeting was not to hire me, but to encourage and show me that the path to finding a job had not been blocked but led right around the corner. I just had to keep taking the steps in faith to get there.

Melissa Stearns was her name. Hardly had she introduced herself, than my nerves and stuttering were a hot mess. She sensed that when she started the interview and told me to relax. Normally someone telling me that would frustrate me, but it felt different coming from her. She went on to tell me that I had nothing to be nervous about, and, because she shared her office with another woman, she asked her colleague to step out during the interview.

She turned off the lights, and we had the interview with only the light from outside lighting our space. She explained that their company had a Bible study every Wednesday and, no matter what was going on and what work everyone had, if they were in the office, they were a part of the Bible study. I thought that was interesting. There was something about being around God's people that made me feel they would see my heart before they let my speech speak for me. It was different, but I knew I wanted to be a part of it.

Melissa then told me that the minister who led their Bible study was Rev. Hardge. I was shocked. Not only did I know Rev. Hardge, my mom considered her one of her godmothers. I had always joked that Rev. Hardge was my homie and would be the minister to give the eulogy at my funeral because she kept it real and kept it short. Rev. Hardge has since passed away, but at that moment I knew even more that I wanted to be a part of whatever this company had going on. Melissa told me she saw something in me and that my being there and interviewing with her was a blessing. She said she saw past my stuttering, and she saw God doing amazing things in my life. I started crying, the second time an interview made me cry but for far greater and better reasons than the first.

I always judged myself on my stuttering, even before others did, wondering if they could understand what I was saying and connect my thoughts because of all the blocks. At this point in my life, my stuttering stuck out to me like a dislocated shoulder because it was the only thing preventing me from getting a job. And here this woman was saying she not only understood me but saw greater things that God would do for me far beyond my just working in her office. I did not have much hope back then. I wondered if I would ever get a job. I went to bed crying some nights, thinking I would be a burden to my family, and I would be letting them down. This interview gave me hope; for that I would be forever indebted. Melissa and I both cried. I honestly do not even remember her asking me too many more questions after that. We hugged and I left thinking that I would surely get the job, but even if I did not, I had more hope than when I walked in that I would get something soon, somewhere.

After not hearing from Ekon for some time, I decided to follow up and inquire about my status. I was told they had hired someone else. I was (somewhat surprisingly, I admit) OK with that. I knew I still had the high possibility of the other job. A couple weeks went by from the home healthcare interview and I reached out asking the status of that job. Melissa said she would call me after I left EarthDance, and that she did. As I walked out of the house, where I worked every day, she called to tell me I had gotten the job. I was happy. Actually, happy does not begin to describe my feelings. YEARS of trying to find a job had finally paid off, and I was going to be working in my field, using my degree, and making just as much as the black girl from grad school! I could not even believe it. I cried yet again, and posted this status to Facebook:

> *Eight months ago, I had an interview where a man told me he would not hire me because of my stuttering. He said, "Hiring you would be like throwing you into the lion's den. The people you would be communicating with would chew you up." His job rejection was one of over 30 in the past 2 years. In December, I received a 6-month internship but I was very low-key about it because I was determined to come out of the internship with a career. Today, I just accepted the job offer to be the Accountant for a healthcare company. I am forever indebted to this company because they looked beyond my speech impediment and saw my desire to work and my knowledge in the field. Around my 24th birthday last month, I*

told my pops I wanted to be a homeowner by 25. I am one step
closer to making that happen! God is so good, y'all.

I texted my whole family and all my friends and threw myself a mini-celebration in my car. FINALLY! Melissa told me they would get back to me with a start date soon. I withdrew my application from the Peace Corps, stopped all my job searches, and prepared myself for this new beginning. Ekon emailed me a few days later asking if I was available after all because they again had an opening. I declined because I had this new job.

A couple of days went by and I had not heard anything more from Melissa. Then a couple of weeks had now passed, so I decided to reach out. To my horror, Melissa told me they had decided not to hire anyone for the position at the moment. Now, devastated was not the word that would come close to describing my feelings. I had resigned from my Plan B Peace Corps option, given up the internship offer with Ekon Benefits, and now was back at square one after telling everyone I had a job.

I did not stay down for long, though. I decided to reach out to Ekon regarding the internship, praying as I typed an email saying that I was available after all and if they still had the position open I would take it. An hour or so later I checked my email to find that not only was the position available, but I could start after my planned, upcoming family vacation. It pays to keep that connection to God and be proactive in hard times instead of reactive. I still had a job. Not the job I wanted—yet again—but one where I needed to be.

My first day at Ekon I managed to not only walk into, but use, the men's restroom! My first week at Ekon I successfully managed to fall down the stairs! Other than those two gaffes, I would say my introduction to corporate America was a success. I was nervous, but that quickly subsided. Being that Ekon was a small company, I did not have many coworkers to introduce myself to. Plus, The Boss's Daughter (and my supervisor), TBD, took me around on the first day and introduced me to my new colleagues. As the introductions concluded and she gave me my first-day paperwork to fill out in her office, TBD asked how I wanted to handle letting everyone know I stuttered. She suggested that she send an email out to everyone, if I was OK with it, explaining that I stutter. I said that, yes, I was OK with it. I did not really know how to handle the situation myself and I wanted to not come across as ignorant since this was my first "big girl" job. TBD sent out the email and I felt somewhat embarrassed, but everyone was understanding and great about the situation.

I remember the first week at lunch I went to the kitchen to eat and the 11:30 lunch-group ladies were already up there enjoying their lunch. They had all been there over 10 years, so they were pretty comfortable with each other. I sat at the table next to them with my headphones on, music on low, and my lunch. They were reading magazines, talking about celebrity gossip, and just generally chatting away. The youngest member of the group—actually, it was more like a clique—was talking about one celebrity in particular and ended the conversation mentioning a speech pattern he had, something along the lines of a lisp or some other speech impediment. I cannot remember exactly. I do remember the eldest of that lunch group trying to be as discreet as possible and mouth the words to be more considerate considering the fact that I had my own speech impediment. I did not acknowledge that I heard them or was able to decipher the mouthed words, but I did allow myself an internal smile.

While I never wanted anyone to pity me or treat me like an abused puppy, it was nice to know the lunch-group ladies were making an effort to be conscious of my stuttering and to not offend me. My family and I often cracked jokes about my stuttering, but I was too new for them to know that.

When I first started my job, I wanted to make a concerted effort to improve my speech so that it would not hinder me. It was during this effort that Chuckie's comedian persona kicked into high gear. I found a stuttering support group that met once a week and, since I was not comfortable going alone, I asked him and my mom to accompany me. I told them the group ran from 6:30 P.M. to 8 P.M. Chuckie said it would last until midnight because no one would be able to get any words out. That is the lighthearted mindset of my family about my stuttering.

Many of my less-enviable personality traits come from my stuttering—my impatience, my quick temper, my moodiness. These flaws that I have, I recognize them. I am impatient because I constantly have to wait on myself to talk. I hate repeating myself because that takes more time. I am short-tempered because it is frustrating knowing what you want to say but not having it come out. When it does come out, it does not get articulated as eloquently as I would like because I try to hide my stuttering or say as little as possible to get the point across with the least amount of stuttering possible. I am moody because my stuttering is moody: one day I can be as fluent as a person who does not stutter; another day, I can stutter as if I am trapped in an endless interview loop.

Just as some of my less-appealing traits are tied up with my stuttering, stuttering has also contributed to some of my strengths. For example, I love the real in people. I like to get to the heart of them and see past the surface. In all my unsuccessful interviews (unsuccessful for the companies because they lost an amazing employee), the interviewers only saw my surface. They saw my stuttering. They showed me what not to do when meeting people, and that is judge them on their flaws.

Stuttering has attracted me to the things that most people consider imperfections, like gaps in teeth or a lisp. I see beauty in blemishes. Perfect is boring. A while ago I read about the Japanese art of Kintsugi, in which broken pieces of pottery or ceramics are repaired with gold, making the items more valuable than they were in their original form. When I first read about Kintsugi I did not think much of it. Then I began to appreciate how every decision we make has consequences, some of which are positive, some negative. I thought about how if we always made the right decision, we would be that original piece of pottery. But every time we mess up, it is an opportunity to learn, gain wisdom, and add value to ourselves. We get a chance to fill our cracks with gold, making us stronger and better than before. As Maya Angelou said: "I can be changed by what happens to me, but I refuse to be reduced by it." So instead of being reduced by my stuttering, I choose to fill my cracks with gold. The "gold" in my stuttering is that it has forced me to be confident.

The only real insecurity I have is my stuttering. Everything else that the world would deem unattractive, I place on a pedestal: this natural hair of mine, my chocolate skin, having minimal curves as a black woman where my culture admires the opposite. This "normal" that the world tries to indoctrinate us about is not the standard unless we deem it so. Normal is not fluency. Normal is not light skin and curves and wavy hair. Normal is relative, and we must begin to welcome that in order to accept ourselves just the way we are.

I realized early on that the limits I placed on myself as far as answering the phone or speaking to clients had spilled over into my supervisor's thoughts and caused her to doubt my capabilities to move onward and upward within the office. My responsibilities began with learning the very basics of retirement plans: contributions, distributions, and the like. While my job duties ultimately increased over the time I was there, they were never anything that required education or creative thinking. Rather, they were simply a matter of following procedures. To compensate for that dreary routine, I began to study for my credentials in the retirement plan industry. Part of what drove me, again, was the mentality that I had to work harder just to be level with a non-stutterer. I began studying and taking the exams. When I told my boss that my goal was to take the exams within a short timeframe, she said, "It is highly unlikely that you will be able to study for and pass the exams." I thought it inappropriate for her to apply her low standards and unwarranted judgments to my life. I kept her views in mind, though. And to you, the reader, keep them in mind as well.

I stayed at Ekon for two-plus years, and in that period I dealt as best I could with my coworkers' ignorance in relation to my stuttering. Eventually, the head of the company entrusted me with the responsibility to lead a large project involving the benefits of an entire work union. Just getting this set up was an enormous task. For example, brainstorming ideas about procedures was hard because my stutter made me less vocal, especially in business settings. While I had a "seat at the table," I was typically reserved rather than vocal out of fear that in speaking I would slow the conversation down and waste people's time. That actually happened once when the company CEO had a meeting to attend, and I was not able to quickly articulate my thoughts and ideas. We were on a time crunch that he and I both felt. We both ended up frustrated, he from the miscommunication, and I from not being able to communicate much at all. But the job was completed. He left for the meeting, and I walked into the bathroom, upset and crying. Upset that I knew what I wanted to say to him, yet my stutter silenced me because the pressure to talk made it worse. Combined with the other times I let my stutter silence me because I chose to be quiet instead of speaking up, it seemed as though I was in a no-win situation.

For the union benefits project, I was the lead person among a group of four, and I made sure to involve the three others in the process and in how to work everything in case a union worker or client called with questions. One of the people in the group was my age. The other two, were in their 40s.

My relationship with my coworkers was always a bit distant. As mentioned, they were very clique-y. The company was nearing 30 years when I started, and the older two ladies had been there nearly 20 of those years. The coworker my age was fairly new compared to them, but her father (who was also an employer and client in the project I was spear-heading) was old friends with Ekon's founder. Somehow, it seemed, everyone was connected, except for me.

I was also the only black person at the company. This was nothing new for me though. I was used to being one of the only, if not the only, black persons in business or higher-level situations such as graduate school as well. While that was never an issue at Ekon, my stuttering did become an issue as tension rose within the project. First, it was the coworker my age who asked to be removed from the endeavor. She had seemed a bit frustrated with project from the beginning, and eventually her role all but disappeared. But I still worked with the older ladies, though at one point, the tension became so thick that we had a meeting to try to clear the air. While I do not recall all the events of the meeting, I do recall my quiet observation, essentially listening and nothing more. At one point, one of the ladies began expressing her frustrations, going so far as to mention that my not talking on the phone because of my stuttering was a hindrance to her. What was interesting about her comment is that all through my schooling in my younger years when I would have expected kids to be cruel, I do not recall blatant disrespect or bullying about my speech. It was not until I became older that I had to deal with that level of disrespect. My coworker said that it was harder for her to do her job because she had to answer the phone, but since she was not doing the day-to-day work like I was, she claimed she could not effectively handle the phone calls. My coworker knew my issue. She knew that the reason she was even part of this project and in this meeting was because of the communication required with the clients, but the part of the communication I could not control was my stuttering. She chose to hit below the belt. My only response to her jab was to smile and chuckle. Unlike her job and career, I knew that where I was at that moment was not my be-all and end-all.

I once read a book by Sister Souljah where the main character was locked up. She had to deal with the guards and older inmates treating her as less than human at times. Instead of getting mad and giving her tormentors the satisfaction of a response, she gave herself wisdom through her thoughts. "Stay calm. Make moves quietly. Let your pride go so you can get your goals accomplished." I did just that. I left the meeting, and the two older ladies, who only conveniently liked each other when they had a common issue, communed at one of their desks (right next to mine) and began whispering about how quiet I was the whole meeting. Of course, they never mentioned how quiet I was in the workplace on a regular basis. Now, though, it was an issue. I am sure they wanted me to hear but also wanted me to think they were trying to be inaudible. I remember thinking their behavior was more infantile than kids my own age back in the days when I was in grade school.

Behavior like that made me all the readier to find a new place of employment. Worse, it was not isolated to the members on my project team. I recall one instance where I was in the kitchen area, preparing a mid-day snack. I ran into our front-desk/marketing specialist, a young woman who loved to talk. She was super friendly, but you know when you are just trying to get in and get out of some place and you get held up but try to be pleasant so as not to be rude to the offending individual? Well, that was me. While the topic of our—of her—conversation was not important, what was important was her reaction after she asked me a question. I proceeded to respond, but midway through I got caught up on a word. She stood there for a moment waiting for me to finish, and then out of nowhere she turned around and walked away. I stood there more confused than shocked or offended. I am almost certain she probably thought I was finished talking, but if she had actually been listening to me speak, she would have known that I was just in mid-sentence. Instead, she turned on her heels as I was stuck on a word and walked back to her desk. Definitely one of the more interesting encounters brought on by my stuttering.

Luckily, I did not stay at that job forever. After dealing with TBD talking with her back to me on numerous occasions when I walked into her office, and after overhearing her proudly proclaiming to be a bitch toward me to a co-worker of mine, I was more than ready to go. But I dreaded the thought of having to start the job-hunting process all over again. It was only after two years at Ekon that I made the decision to look for another place of employment. My prior job hunt was in the back of my mind upon beginning the search again. Would I be another three years trying to find a new job, all the while stuck in my current job, until I could move onward and upward in my career? I asked myself. The thought of staying comfortable (I use the word loosely, what with having to deal with TBD) was worse than stuttering through another round of interviews. So, putting my misgivings aside, I resolved to restart the quest.

I utilized the same websites and processes I had used two years before, only this time there was not as much pressure as I already had a job. Going into interviews I always told myself, "Relax. Even if you do not get this, you still have a job and an income." Having that Plan B made it easier to go into interviews and not stutter as much as I would have if I'd desperately needed a job. I still stuttered greatly because interviews always increase my nerves, but the stutter was not intensified by my dire need for a job as it had been in my previous job searches. I went on a few interviews, nowhere near as many as I had in the past. Four or five, max, within a 3-to-4-month period. The interesting thing was that in all those interviews, I was the one reaching out trying to find the job—until one day I received a message on LinkedIn from a recruiter.

The talent acquisition specialist and recruiter at a St. Louis-area accounting firm reached out to me saying my background and work experience were a match for a job for which she was recruiting. I did a little background research of my own on the company website, looked at the position, and believed it was not just a match but a perfect match. Not only that, it was a natural progression from the work I was doing at Ekon. It was the work I wanted to do at Ekon, but TBD and my coworkers were too scared to give me that responsibility because they did not know how to make it work with my stuttering. I immediately replied to the recruiter and told her yes, I would be interested in an interview. I set it up and within a week I was sitting before a partner and the principal of the firm.

Before the interview, I informed them that I stutter, as I typically did for my job interviews. The thing I remember that was different about them was that they told me it was OK, that there was nothing to be nervous about, and that it would not be a problem. When I got to the interview, I was calmer than normal. That said, my stuttering turned into a hot mess once I got in the room with them. The interview started with just the principal, Michelle, who asked me to tell her about myself, the typical interview question. Once she saw the extent of my stutter, it immediately became less of a conversation, and more her doing most of the talking. She told me about the company, how they operated, and that the partner would be arriving shortly once he was finished with another meeting. She then told me that her brother stuttered. At that moment a lightbulb went off in me and something told me that I would get the job. It was not the simple fact that her brother stuttered, but I knew that because she had experience with someone close to her stuttering, she would understand how stuttering worked. She would understand that stuttering did not affect my mental capacity, as so many other people seemed to think. She would understand that I could talk, it just took longer. She would understand that I could do the job.

After she finished talking about all of the particulars of the job, Patrick, the partner, walked in. She filled him in on what we had discussed, and then he asked me a few questions such as, "What career path do you see for yourself?" and "What salary would you want to make?" But it was the final question he asked that stood out the most and that no other potential employer had ever asked me in an interview. He did not dance around the fact that I stuttered, and he was straightforward in saying that it would be different for them. He then asked me, "Since we are not used to working with someone who stutters, what requests would you have of us to be able to accommodate you?" I was thrown off by that question because I had never had a possible employer ask me how they could work with me. I mean, they had already found me on LinkedIn. But now they were asking how they could work with me. I thought for a split second and replied, "Just be patient with me." Patrick said, "Fair enough."

I left the interview feeling extremely confident. In the days after, I thanked Michelle and Patrick for the interview, followed up a couple of times, and waited for the phone call that would let me know I had been hired. I was that confident. Thus, you can imagine my surprise when they informed me they had decided to go in another direction, for the time being, and I did not get the position, though they said they would let me know if something came up in the future. To be honest, I was hurt. When I did not get other positions, I was unaffected, but this was different. Nonetheless, I accepted it and decided to just focus on finishing my exams for my credentials instead of pursuing other job opportunities.

For about two months, I continued working and studying for my credentials. One day, I received an email from the recruiter who had reached out to me earlier. She had initially called me, but because I was at work and did not recognize the number, I did not answer. When I checked my email about an hour later, there was a message from her to call her back. I got excited, but I also wished I had answered the phone when she originally called. Now I would have to make a phone call, and the thought of that stressed me out. I got up the nerve to finally call her about two hours later. By that time, it was the end of the work day and no one answered. Huge sigh of relief. I then emailed her to let her know I had called. She wrote back saying she was leaving for the day but would call the next business day. It was Friday. Not only was it Friday, it was Labor Day weekend. Whatever she had to tell me, it would have to wait four days until she got back to the office on Tuesday. I told my dad and Wade in a text about the interaction. Wade said she would not leave me hanging for days on end if there would not ultimately be good news. I hoped he was correct, and I made my way to Chicago to enjoy my own Labor Day weekend.

I hung out with my friends three relaxing days. On Sunday, we made our way to church. I almost did not go because I was too tired, but Brandon, an original member of The Crew from my college days who had become one of my closest male friends, was not really letting my stay-in-bed choice be an option. So, to church we went. Of course, the pastor's sermon seemed to speak to me. Again, because I have the memory of a granny, I do not recall the exact message, but I remember his saying in the next 48 hours, we were going to receive that blessing breakthrough. Brandon knew about my pending phone call with the recruiter, so we both kind of looked at each other and acknowledged that this was my sign. Just as Wade predicted and the preacher proclaimed, the blessing came through on Tuesday morning! I accepted a job offer to become a retirement plan specialist at Benefit Plans Plus, LLC (BPP).

As ready as I was to leave my current place of employment, I decided not to leave them high and dry during our busy season and with the new project that had caused so much tension in the first place. My plan was to start the new job a month out from when I accepted the offer. Per proper procedure, I informed my bosses of my intent to leave. First, I told the big boss. He was sad to see me go. Honestly, he was one of the better things about the job. I had and still do have a lot of respect for him. He built the company over 30 years, employing nearly 20 people, and works there to this day. He told me he appreciated my being a member of the Ekon team and that my stuttering had brought a new dimension to the workplace. He felt my stuttering had not only benefitted him, but also benefitted the employees. To work with someone who stutters, he said, taught everyone patience and acceptance. I almost started crying when I met with him. His daughter, on the other hand, was a different story.

When I told TBD I was leaving, her response was cold, and her only concern was my returning the study materials that I had been using to get my credentials. After meeting with her, I went to lunch. When I got back from lunch, I saw that she had taken the check scanner from my desk. It had been my duty to handle the daily check deposits, but not anymore! My dad said he thought it was in my best interest, so in case anything came up fishy during my transition, I could not be held to blame. Still, TBD's sneaky act freed me from any guilt I may have had (which, to be honest, was slim to none, anyway) about going to work for a competitor. Speaking of guilt (or lack thereof), on the sixteenth of October, I finished clearing out my desk and departed the office without so much as a goodbye to TBD. Never have I felt more at peace with a decision in my life.

With my new job, I did not have many nerves about my stutter. The first day, Michelle walked me around and introduced me to everyone, which saved a ton of awkward introductions. As far as handling the work, the format of the job allowed me to work my best without having to worry about the communications aspect. As what is known as a third-party administrator (TPA) on retirement plans—if you work at a job with a 401(k), then I am the person behind the scenes who oversees the technicalities of that plan—I calculated contributions, ensured contributions complied with Internal Revenue Service regulations, filed tax forms with the Department of Labor, and made sure the plans were in compliance with the plan document and the IRS. A major issue that I ran into at my prior job in dealing with clients was no longer an issue at BPP. Communicating with clients on my behalf always seemed to stress my former co-workers out, but the set-up at BPP was two people per client, thus eliminating the issue altogether. This was just another confirmation that BPP was where I was supposed to be.

Things were running smoothly, which is how you know you are meant to be somewhere. The issues I had at Ekon were nowhere to be seen. Where I had to search out my last job, this job found me. Even though they told me no initially after the interview, they came back and hired me. Where my previous coworkers treated my stuttering as a burden at times, Michelle was trying to find ways to make me feel included. In meetings, she suggested I bring my laptop and IM my thoughts and suggestions so I would feel comfortable. When clients called and left voicemails, my coworkers did not mind returning the calls on my behalf. Once, when a new employee started at the firm, some of my coworkers and I were having a conversation. The new employee asked me my age. It took me a while to respond, and she said, "Cat got your tongue? You forget your age?" Without hesitation, one of the other employees who was in conversation with us said, "Just wait a minute. Your answer is coming." It was that kind of support that I truly appreciated, especially in comparison to my experience at Ekon, where people resorted to whispering about my not speaking up instead of speaking up on my behalf. Yes, I can talk. But sometimes it is good to know someone has your back. Overall, I never felt (and still do not feel) that my stuttering was holding me back in my current position. As I move up, communication will be more on the forefront, but I will cross that bridge when I come to it.

CHAPTER SIX

Stutter-stepping on the Way to the Top

When I started writing this book, I had just entered the world of corporate America. I had just received the job offer at the healthcare company—before being told I did not have the job after all. As I thought I had finally made it, I started writing about how God had blessed me with this situation and how it seemingly had fallen into my lap. It has been a pattern in my life that the path I am supposed to take usually makes itself clear because even though I have put in the work, the situation comes easily and flows seamlessly into my life, just as my current job found me on LinkedIn without my putting in any effort to find it.

I started writing the book because I wanted to share that job-hunt journey and the moments that were part of it that would stick with me forever. I wanted to share about the time when I moved back to my dad's house after grad school and was rejected by employer after employer, so I enlisted the help of my stepmom's human resource co-worker who gave me a practice interview. In that interview she said I should always look interviewers in the eye, and then she asked me to answer her next question making eye contact. I rarely made eye contact with people because it made me uncomfortable since I stuttered. I never admitted this to anyone, and those times I tried to maintain eye contact through my stutter, I would end up crying, ashamed that I could not do something as simple as looking others in the eye.

I started writing because I wanted to include all the funny situations I have been in, such as taking my dog to the veterinarian and trying to sign him in for his appointment. I could not get King's name out, causing the doctor to rush from around the counter because she thought I was having a stroke or was about to faint. I wanted to write about the time I visited my dad and made a grocery-store stop only to run into the speech pathologist my dad used to take me to at the hospital. Except we did not actually run into each other because I saw her and made a swift U-turn to a different cashier to avoid sparking up a conversation with her that only showed I still stuttered and the years of attending therapy with her had been in vain.

I wanted to write about the moments as a kid when I thought I had outsmarted my parents and successfully got my dad to sign me up for sign-language classes. I showed major interest because a friend of mine from summer camp was deaf, but, deep down, I only showed such interest because I figured I would learn sign language and never have to talk again! I realized that learning sign language and all the words was a lot harder than I thought it would be, especially at elementary-school age, and stuttering was a lot easier than all the learning I would have to put in.

I wanted to share my moments of growing up with a stutter and having other kids think I was bougie or stuck up because I would not talk to them, but really, I was just reserved because I knew that being called those names was better than being laughed at when they heard me talk. I wanted to share how stuttering made me quiet and self-reliant.

I started writing this book to share all those experiences, though they did not seem that deep back then. I did not see my journey as a testimony, just as my life. Everyone has something they have been through, so I did not think what I had been through would touch as many people as it has. And I did not think it would affect my personal growth as much as it has.

I never thought that when I started writing this book I would be where I am today. I never thought I would have started a YouTube channel where the main focus is my stutter and where I expose that insecurity to the world. Through YouTube I have reached the four corners of the globe, from Italy and France to Nigeria and South Africa, from India to Brazil.... The goal of the YouTube channel was to connect with other stutterers because I always felt alone growing up, and it was my hope that some kid would see my video and know they were not alone.

When I was growing up, YouTube was not what it is today. So, to be able to represent such a small percentage of people—those who stutter—on a global scale, I do not take that opportunity lightly. I have received messages from speech pathologists saying they showed their young clients my videos and told them, "One day you can be a YouTube star like Matice." I received a message from a young man who told me his stutter often had him contemplating suicide, but I gave him hope that his impediment did not have to dictate his life in such a heavy manner. I have had young black girls send me messages that say they have never met another black woman who stuttered; I inspired them to come out of their shell and not hide their stutter as they once did. While my goal was to offer encouragement to stutterers, I have also educated non-stutterers and helped parents and spouses cope with and be better able to appropriately respond to their loved ones' speech. And then there are the people who have no relation to stuttering who are inspired by my willingness to be so open and vulnerable in sharing my stutter with the world. What started as something small has touched the lives of many. To the man at my graduate school alma mater who said people would chew me up because of my stutter: As I write this, 24,000 people have subscribed to my channel on YouTube, and I have not been chewed up yet, nor will I ever.

And not only have I *touched* lives all over the world, I am able to *travel* all over the world. When I first heard about my graduate school coworker making $60,000, I would dream of the places I would be able to visit on a salary like that. I used to imagine the white, sandy beaches of Greece and the colorful markets in Morocco. I used to pray that I could travel to just one of these countries. Now? I just got back from Turks and Caicos, the tenth international country I have visited!

I was once admiring my stepmom's wedding ring, and I told her I could not wait to have a ring with a rock that size. She said, "Never wait on a man before you get to have your own diamonds." I took that to heart and a step further. When I turned 25, and seven months into my internship at Ekon Benefits, I promised to give myself the world and not let my stuttering hold me back from communicating in a foreign country. Now that I had the means to travel, thanks to a job I never thought I would have, I was not about to live anything but my best life. As you can see, I am most definitely not waiting for those diamonds! And now, I can tell funny stories about getting stopped in customs at the airport and receiving hesitant, suspicious looks from the security officers because they mistook my stutter as someone who was lying, and a possible threat entering their country.

Now I am working for a company that supported my job and professional credential pursuits. Not only was I able to attain my credentials in the time I said I would, I went further and attained the next credential up from that. In all, there was a total of six exams, and I passed every one of them on the first try. So, to my former boss who told me it was highly unlikely that I would pass, I not only did what I said I would, I did it with the highest possible scores.

It is important to me that this book not be some feel-good story with a fairy-tale ending. I know there are more hard days to come. I have had to deal with hecklers on the internet telling me I am embarrassing myself by making videos and wishing I would hurry up and talk. I have had to self-reflect and realize that it is not always someone else's responsibility in the workplace to "save me" from situations such as using the phone or dealing with clients. And I have had to admit that some of the concerns at my prior job were warranted, no matter how rudely they were conveyed to me.

I have had to ask myself, "Why can I not be patient with other people when everyone has to be patient with me?" Why do I expect something from others that I so rarely give them? I have had to realize that my impatience with the improvement process via speech therapy may have been what delayed my blessing in the form of the jobs and traveling.

I have asked myself, "What if I no longer stuttered?" A former teacher of mine said he used to stutter until one day his father scared him so badly on the farm he grew up on that his stutter went away. What if my stutter miraculously went away; who would I be without it? Do I even want to speak fluently? It is interesting asking myself these questions because I truly do not know the answers. But I do know that God does not put more on us than we can handle, and I would rather have to deal with this than be someone who may not be able to face the light of day with their stutter. I would rather be the one to deal with the struggle because I know I am strong enough to handle it.

This strength and resiliency did not happen overnight, and it is not always as present as I would like it to be. But if there is one message that resonates in this book, I hope it is that what society deems as normal does not have to be the standard for our life.

So many people think that my stutter is not normal. I see comments all the time on my YouTube channel from people who say listening to me makes them want to cry or that they feel so bad for me or they hope I can overcome my situation. My message to them is that even if I never stop stuttering and even if I do not have a single fluent day for the rest of my life, I am going to be OK, as evidenced by the fulfilling life I am living now.

"Normal" to a fluent speaker is fluency. Normal to me is stuttering. And, yes, it is hard some days, but even fluent speakers have their insecurities and struggles; they just are not on display for the world to criticize or sympathize with. Normal is relative, and while stuttering may be different, it is no less normal for me and for others who stutter.

I am grateful for this journey of being able to support and give confidence to people who stutter, and I am grateful for being a positive representation of what living with a disability can look like. I had a man tell me I did not appear to be the kind of person who would stutter, so I am proud to be able to break down the stereotypes and misconceptions that come with stuttering, and with disabilities in general. But what I am most grateful for are the people in my life who allow me to be 100 percent myself. I am grateful that my dad has finally come around and let me stutter in peace without my feeling that underlying, constant pressure of needing to improve. I am grateful that my mom is still always there, ready to protect me and step in if need be, even as she allows me my voice and my independence. I am grateful for my siblings and step-parents, who always wait patiently for me to get my words out, and for my friends who never judge me or are embarrassed to be with me because of my stutter. The way I see it, if this natural-haired, dark-skinned, stuttering black woman can infiltrate corporate America without letting her crown fall, then the sky is the limit. I am stutter stepping all the way to the top!

CHAPTER SEVEN

Selflessness*

(*writings from my closest family and friends)

Wade F. Morris Sr. (Pops)

Exactly when Matice began to stutter is a blur. Nonetheless, at the time it became apparent that her stuttering was not a phase, she was living in St. Louis with her mother, and I had limited contact with her. That would have been when she was in second or third grade. During the time she was living in St. Louis, I would encourage her to slow down her speech and think about what she wanted to say. That method did not work because she became frustrated with me for constantly encouraging her to slow down.

My opportunity to have daily contact with Matice came when she moved in with us as she was about to enter sixth grade. Around

Christmas of that year my wife, Julie, suggested that we take Matice to a speech therapist because my methods were having no impact on Matice's stuttering. By the end of January of sixth grade, Matice was receiving speech therapy one day a week from outside of the school and another session with a different therapist through the school district. Matice never really said much about the therapy sessions, and I did not say much about them to her. I would converse with the private therapist after each session. Those conversations would center on the strategies that they worked on and what was supposed to occur before the next session.

During those three years of middle school (sixth through eighth grade) Matice's stuttering only mildly improved. About 18 months into the process, the private therapist told me that Matice should be improving significantly more than what she had shown.

In my conversations with Matice, it appears that she does not believe that she can overcome her stuttering. She seems to believe that stuttering is something that cannot be resolved, as if she were broken and cannot be fixed. Regardless of how often, or in what manner I told her that she could learn to speak fluently, she refused to accept my suggestion.

After middle school, Matice moved back to St. Louis with her mother. While she was in high school, undergrad, and graduate school, I tried different methods to push Matice to use her strategies to help her speak fluently. I made promises and bribed her to get her to use the strategies. None of those methods of encouragement were successful. Matice would start using them but then abandon them after a few days, for whatever reason. She does not stutter when she sings (albeit badly) or when she is angry. Several of my many conversations with Matice to overcome stuttering were to develop a flow to what she says, as though she were singing. She had, absolutely, no interest in working on that strategy.

It has always pained me to listen to Matice stutter. I want the best for her, and I realized that stuttering could be a road block. When I listened to Matice struggle to read a passage aloud when she went to her private speech therapist, I wanted to cry. It took her no less than two minutes to read the passage that should have taken less than half that time. From what I have seen, she avoids certain situations that would cause her to speak to people because she is self-conscious about her stuttering. I often wondered if she was being bullied in school or if she was avoiding talking in school because of her stuttering.

At this point (Matice is 28 years old as I write this), her stuttering is out of my hands. She has a good job and is doing well in that job. I cannot let my frustration with her stuttering interfere with my relationship with Matice. Any advances that Matice makes to speak fluently will be a result of her desire to do so. Regardless of my efforts, she has accepted that she cannot overcome her stuttering.

Denita E. Robinson (Momma)

A Lesson in Patience and Grace

Trying to summarize 28 years of living with your child who is categorized with a speech disability, which to me is our normal, is quite challenging. But for the sake of NOT being replaced as her manager (lol), I thought I would give it my yeoman's best. Here goes...

At the initial revelation by an observant educator, I did what any good mother (who's also an educator) would do—that is, follow up on the recommendation to have my daughter assessed. The results were astounding: OCD (obsessive-compulsive disorder) with tics. Supposedly, the OCD and tics also led to the stuttering due to the manner in which her brain registered information.

Since I was familiar with this particular disorder, I was not majorly alarmed. I did further research and, more important, studied my daughter on a daily basis. It was in the midst of this regime that I realized this was something that could potentially be managed and/or outgrown. As a loving mother, optimist and believer that Matice could just "fix it," I thought we would easily get through this. I thought, since she was on the mild end of the spectrum, that this would be easy. Boy, was I ever wrong!

I went from euphoric SUPERMOM thoughts (I can fix this) to a gamut of defeatist thoughts and emotions, some of which I am revealing publicly for the very first time.

The truth of the matter is:

I was in major denial.

I constantly sought cures and remedies.

I failed miserably trying to support.

I felt total guilt.

I prayed consistently for a reprieve.

I prayed for total deliverance.

I accepted this as God's plan.

I saw a greater vision.

I realized there is purpose to the pain.

I finally entered a place of peace.

My daughter's stuttering journey has affected our relationship in so many ways, defining who we are and our relationship today. To say the journey has been difficult would be an understatement. It has been trying, troubling, frustrating, and downright enraging at times, but I honestly would not have done things any other way. Every struggle has strengthened us. Every mishap has provided a mission for us. And every misstep has rerouted us to this moment.

In spite of its being Matice who has lived with the disability and experienced pain I know nothing about, I feel as though I had the greatest lessons to learn. Why? As a parent, you do not want to see your child suffer or endure hardship and hurt. Knowing the propensity of others who knew about her speech impediment to mistreat her, or her classmates and peers to be cruel—even rejecting her and making her an outcast—I was always in protective mode. I constantly made suggestions and recommendations, thinking I was comforting and reassuring her. Eventually, I had to learn to take a back seat to her navigating and advocating for herself.

Learning to follow her lead, as opposed to taking the lead, was for me possibly the most rewarding outcome of this disorder. From elementary to high school to freshman year of college, the IEP was my tool to proactively protect my child against any academic difficulties. Socially, though, we were on our own. I am very proud of Matice's commitment to being abnormally normal! For me, it has been a lesson in patience and experiencing God's grace.

Watching closely from the wings, I never failed to be amazed and proud of how beautifully Matice handled herself. Whether it was rude characters on the phone or ignorant characters in person, she had a winning attitude. On those occasions when she needed assistance (such as making doctor appointments), I was there. Not always without being too insistent (the sign of epic frustration—and insensitivity—on my part) or being fussed at by her (me doing what I thought she'd told me, but adding my own twist, she says), but we made it.

There is so much more that I want to say, but I'll simply say this: Matice's disability has given her the greatest ability . . . she is a thinker wise beyond her years! Her silence is a deadly weapon. Her speech (whether fluent, articulate or not) is impressive. As with most individuals who compensate for a deficit in one area of their life, Matice's communication skills (particularly her writing skills) have been strengthened to where they are at the superior level. But her greatest accomplishment, in my opinion, is the fact that she has traveled the globe and chosen to live her best life in the face of what has hindered many in similar circumstances.

I am her greatest fan and number one encourager. I look forward to sharing her with the world! Go, Big Meech, go!

Love,

Momma

Walter "Chuck" Robinson (stepdad)

When I first met Matice, I thought her stuttering was cute. Initially, when she would speak, it appeared as if she was so serious or crying. I say that because her eyes would close and her face would contort. I would always make a joke about it, telling her that her eyes would eventually roll back in her head.

At the same time, I would tease her about how she never seemed to stutter when she was going off on people. So, I would jokingly say to her, "I need to make you mad more often!" We always laughed, but we also recognized that there was a measure of truth in that statement.

On a more serious note, her stuttering would also pull at my heartstrings. I would always pray and ask God to deliver her from that struggle and make her life smoother as it relates to communicating.

I distinctly remember a moment while we were standing in the kitchen during a time when she was looking for a job. She was extremely frustrated. She felt her stuttering was impeding her ability to become gainfully employed. Through her tears, I hugged her, encouraged her, and prayed with her. I also assured her that she would be successful at accomplishing her mission and not to worry about anything. I had her back. If nothing else, I told her she could come and work for me, as I owned my own business.

My faith has always been strong, and it was a necessary entity for her in that moment. I even reminded her that she always had full access to my bankroll (with approval from the Boss, Momma).

I am extremely proud of Matice. I am thankful that God has blessed her and allowed her to be where she is today. I am grateful that God answered her prayer, as she now lives fully without hindrance and with the stuttering.

From her big homie supporter,

Chuckie (AKA Walter Lee)

Julie Morris (stepmom)

When Matice asked us all to write about our experience with her as a stutterer, I was not sure what to write about. Looking back, I guess when she was a child I worried a lot about it and wanted to do everything I could to help her overcome her stuttering. As she grew older and then into adulthood, it became clear to me that she had made a conscious decision to embrace her stuttering as a part of who she is. Whether or not I agree with that decision is neither here nor there because I see my role, as "Julie," to be one who supports her decisions and offers advice when and if she asks me for it. Even though I respect her decision to embrace her stuttering as a part of her, I still worry about that one day when she is the only one to be counted on to communicate in an emergency and she won't be able to do so. What if something tragic happens to someone she loves because she chose to embrace her challenge instead of overcome it?

Wade F. Morris Jr. (older brother)

It is noticed, relentless, and always in your face. Stuttering is the thing that constantly rears its ugly head when talking to my sister, and it has even dictated the manner by which we communicate. Each and every person has some sort of a trial or tribulation they must endure at some point in their life. Some are brief and others are lasting; stuttering is one that seems likely to last a lifetime.

When we were younger, we both had to go to speech therapy. Although it was for different issues, I realized that her problem with stuttering was a much larger obstacle than my pronunciation of "r's" and "s's." After a few years, while I had graduated from the program, Matice was still working to gain control of her speech. As a kid I do not remember my sister's stuttering, but that's not to say it wasn't bad. As we grew older, I constantly bugged her to slow down and enunciate in an exaggerated manner, believing that that would help her regain control as that was what I had been taught. Long story short, we never knew if that worked or would have worked because she refused to do it. Or at least she refused to do it for any significant amount of time that would allow anyone to make a realistic determination.

Today, we are both grown and because I am in the military we only see each other in person about once a year. This means most of our communication is via the phone. We text more than we talk and even though we haven't outright discussed it, her stuttering plays a role in that.

From time to time, I hear stories about some idiot who believes insulting this challenge that she has is funny or demeaning to her. But it is incredible to think that even more than the obviously slower speech, a bigger, perhaps even the biggest, impact that I believe stuttering has had on Matice is in her confidence. She could elect to live a very isolated life socially and professionally, but instead she chooses to thrive. She travels the world, fights for what she deserves at work and is constantly crushing the social scene with friends and family. In other words, her stuttering has not held her back but emboldened her. Because she has gone through it and come out stronger on the other end, she is living one of the fullest lives of anyone I know.

For my sister, I am not entirely sure that she cannot exercise more control over her speech. I believe that if she truly slowed down she would certainly be able to get a better handle on it, but at the end of the day what I want is for her to be happy, comfortable with who she is, and not be held back in any manner due to her speech impediment. So, ultimately, it is what it is, but I think the two things that lead to long and fulfilling lives are humor and genuine happiness. For sure, those are two things she has definitely developed, as she has learned to cope/live with stuttering.

Celene Morris ("Seester")

My sister is not the kind of person you meet and then put out of your mind. Her personality is, in my opinion, unforgettable. She is loud, caring, and dedicated—did I mention she also has beautiful hair and skin? Yes, her stuttering is also part of her personality and, granted, some people remember her by that whether they realize it or not. Her stuttering is a part of her personality in the same way that she embraces her loud self or she embraces her hair and skin: it's part of who she is. A lot of people who stutter work endless hours to change it and they are embarrassed by it, but over the years I think Matice has a different view on her stuttering—and that is something to remember her by.

Tyson Morris (younger brother)

As Matice's younger brother, I can say without a doubt that her stuttering does not affect the way I think about her in any way. After you get used to hearing it, you barely notice it. I did not ever think it was a big deal because I love her and that is all that matters.

Patience Olishile (friend)

I'd never known anyone who stuttered until I met Matice. We have been friends for 10 years and, oh, the times we have had! I cannot pinpoint the first time we met but I am sure it went something along the lines of, "Hey, I'm Patience." To which she replied after a pause, "I'm Matice. I stutter." I am able to recall this conversation verbatim because it's the interaction I've watched my friend have so many times over the years, and I wouldn't think our first interaction was much different. Although it has been a long time since the pause between her thoughts made me feel in any way awkward, I can remember early on in our friendship when it did.

There were times when Matice wanted to tell some amazing story and got so frustrated that she would just say, "Never mind!" or when I knew what she wanted to say (or took it upon myself to assume I knew what she wanted to say) and just wanted to "help her out." There were many times early on that I or someone we knew would play this guessing game of trying to finish her sentences, and Matice would get even more frustrated. At those times I would think, "I'm not doing this to be mean. I just want to help her get it out." As a friend, you never want to see your friends struggle in any way, and it would honestly break my heart to see how uncomfortable it was for her. It made perfect sense to me at the time to try to jump in, but now I have a different outlook on things. While I thought I was helping, I was only adding to the frustration. How would I feel if I were very capable of having an intelligent conversation and because I took a little longer to get the words out people took it upon themselves to tell ME what I was going to say? I wouldn't appreciate it, even if it were coming from a good place.

When we go out in a social setting where we will meet people, Matice packs this "I stutter" phrase in her artillery for the awkward pauses and such that she knows will ensue, as if it were part of her name. It's for those who do not have that experience with a person who stutters and gives that confused look, or for the blatantly ignorant person who might say something that is completely uncalled for. As these interactions began to happen more often, I grew very defensive for my friend. Knowing Matice and how funny and bright she is, it would enrage me that people could be so insensitive and judge her. It was difficult for me to see the conversations play out the way they did, but also, knowing the kind of spitfire she is, I knew she preferred—politely—to put anyone in their place who questioned her intelligence.

As I look over our almost-10-year friendship, I see the growth in Matice. Through the stories I was told prior to our meeting as well as the personal experience I have had, I know that stuttering was a very large hurdle for her, but I can confidently say she has won the battle. Does she still stutter? Yes. Does she come into contact with people who do not quite know how to handle her stuttering? I am sure she does. Does she still face adversity? Yes. But instead of letting the stuttering define how she was going to live her life, the stuttering forced Matice to be more courageous. It is a truly inspiring story. Matice is adventurous, daring, fun loving, carefree, determined, hard-working, persistent and beautiful not only outside but inside as well. When you get to know Matice, the stutter honestly takes a backseat to the amazing, wonderful person she is.

Brandon Barnett (friend)

What is it like to have a friend who stutters? My experience may be different from others'. My father stutters, so in many ways, I am used to it. However, I have found myself to be hyper sensitive to those who stutter. To explain: I have seen people bully others for their speech impediment/disorder throughout life. I even have memories of children, and, sadly, adults, who mocked my father for his stutter. Seeing this has created some uneasiness and a need to protect those with speech disorders. No one deserves mistreatment, especially for something that is beyond their control. But this is the reality and the society we live in. Nevertheless, my experiences with Matice have been interesting, to say the least, particularly dealing with her periods of insecurity and my own hyper sensitivity, both of which have taught me two important lessons.

People tend to be shy or insecure about their speech impediments/disorders. Matice has developed a certain level of self-assurance regarding her stutter. This is clear. She even casually jokes about her stutter from time to time. However, there have been periods where her insecurity has surfaced. In a lighter example, I have never gotten her to participate in a casual game of Taboo or any other word game because she knows/feels she will stutter. But on a more serious note, I remember when Matice entered the job market after attaining her master's in accounting. Imagine spending tens of thousands of dollars, devoting years, months, days, weeks, hours, and minutes studying, and sacrificing relationships among other things, to achieve your academic dream, only to walk into an interview and be denied employment due to a speech disorder. Unfortunately, this was the reality for Matice, and it was a very upsetting time for her. Situations like these are obviously difficulty for anybody. This period was reasonably hard on her family and friends, like myself, albeit to a far lesser degree than they were for Matice.

What kind of advice do you give a friend who will likely be discriminated against because of their speech disorder, or any disability for that matter? How do you comfort a friend who goes to interview after interview to be—and feel—rejected because speaking and communicating to clients and coworkers is an essential part of their profession? When talking to Matice about this, I often wondered if I was giving good advice. These questions ran through my mind each time the subject came up. And it came up a lot. There is no magic word to make someone feel better in a situation like this.

As I have stated, my interactions with Matice helped me discover my own hyper-sensitivities. There have been countless times when Matice and I have been at a restaurant and she would stutter as she began to order. Circumstances like this can easily create a "trifecta" of discomfort in that the server becomes frustrated and agitated, Matice feels uncomfortable trying to place her food order, and I feel uncomfortable because of the discomfort around me. Side note: As I write this, I am wondering if I have been projecting my own discomfort among others all this time. That being the case or not, many's the time I've grappled with whether to step in and help place Matice's order or whether to restrain myself and let her complete the order herself. On the one hand, I want to be helpful, but on the other hand I do not want to be disrespectful or make her feel inadequate. Again, these are thoughts I have pondered. More often than not, I have found myself giving free rein to Matice to complete her own sentences amid her stuttering—especially in public settings. In private, though, there have been times where I have actively encouraged her to use her speech therapy techniques, such as singing her thoughts aloud, to help work through her stutters. But it is situations such as being in restaurants that have taught me the importance of patience.

There are numerous stories I could tell such as the time a friend of mine privately and with all kindness asked me if Matice had Tourette syndrome. I mention this because my friend, Matice and I all shared a laugh about her question. That said, I chose to emphasize the two situations above because they reminded me of the importance of empathy and patience. While empathy and patience can be important in many situations, they are particularly important when interacting with someone with a speech disorder, or any disability. Everyone deserves to be not only understood, but respected. Offering empathy and patience ensures that people with speech disorders, like Matice, are understood and respected.

Darnell King (ex-boyfriend)

A while ago you asked me what it was like to date someone who stuttered. In the beginning it was a little frustrating. You could be so stubborn at times. My memory is vivid when it comes to you. We would go on dates and I remember your trying so hard when ordering dinner. When I said, "Babe, let me order," you snapped at me. That moment exemplified you (And I never tried to order for you again). I embraced everything about you from then on. To me, honestly, stuttering was your best quality.

I remember my sitting on the bed with you and our singing songs and me trying to understand why you could sing and not stutter but not talk and not stutter. I never once criticized you or was embarrassed by you. I only tried to understand. The singing games, though, were the best... and the sentence repeating... you would do so well... and then getting into it with my best friend Terry and us essentially falling out for him joking about it to other friends, but of course I did not play when it came to you. So crazy 'cause your mom texted me the other day and said she was talking to you and she told you I was the only one who tried to understand or embrace your stuttering and help you with it... and then it hit me... how cool we were, and how much we said we loved each other and we do not even communicate anymore…. Not to get off the subject, but your stuttering makes you *you*. Even when you were job hunting and felt you were not getting your due or that companies were scared to take a chance on you, I kept trying to encourage you and tell you it was their loss.

Acknowledgments

I am thankful for my editor, Richard. From our very first meeting you told me you recognized quality when you saw it, and you saw it in me. I am also thankful for your patience and work ethic, especially near the end of this project. I intentionally chose not to have you edit this page just so I could say, *"I truly appreciate all your hard work!"* Do you like the italics?

I am thankful for everyone else who had a hand in helping with this book. To Patrick and Brittney who were the photographer and graphic designer, respectively, thank you for making the vision for my cover come to life. Thank you to Ace for creating my digital book image. Also, thank you to Cedric who gave his time and wisdom regarding the publishing and marketing process.

I am especially thankful for my "Momanager", family, and friends for their input and support while I wrote this book. Y'all are the real MVPs!

About the Author

Matice was born in Killeen, Texas, but has spent much of her life in St. Louis, Mo. She attended the University of Missouri-St. Louis, where she received her Bachelor of Science degree in accounting. She then earned a Master of Science degree in Accounting at the University of Illinois at Chicago. She also received her Qualified 401(k) Administrator (QKA) and Qualified Pension Administrator (QPA) credentials through the American Society of Pension Professionals & Actuaries.

The Product of My Selfishness: The Stutter and the Story is the first book written by Matice. As someone who stutters, she wanted to encourage and educate stutterers and non-stutterers alike about the challenges people who stutter face. Keeping with that same mission, she started a YouTube channel in July 2017 that focuses on how she and others can live their best life with a stutter. Through YouTube, she has a platform that spans six of the seven continents. (She is determined to find someone who stutters in Antarctica!)

Outside of touching hearts and lives with her openness about her stutter, Matice loves adventure and travel. When she is not physically traveling, she likes to "travel" vicariously through the characters in the books she reads. Her favorite authors are Paulo Coelho and Terry McMillan, and her favorite book at the moment is *Homegoing* by Yaa Gyasi.

No matter what she is doing or where she is going, Matice lives by two mottos: "Progress, not perfection," and "Onward and upward." Always, in all ways.

29258469R00079

Made in the USA
Columbia, SC
21 October 2018